PENSION POWER

PENSION POWER

TAKE CONTROL OF YOUR MOST VALUABLE FINANCIAL ASSET

THIRD EDITION

DEBBIE HARRISON

FINANCIAL TIMES
PRENTICE HALL

Pearson Education Limited

Head Office:
Edinburgh Gate
Harlow CM20 2JE
Tel: +44 (0)1279 623623
Fax: +44 (0)1279 431059

London Office:
128 Long Acre
London WC2E 9AN
Tel: +44 (0)171 447 2000
Fax: +44 (0)171 240 5771
www.business-minds.com

First published in Great Britain 1999

ISBN 0 273 64157 3

British Library Cataloguing in Publication Data
A CIP catalogue record for this book can be obtained from the British Library.

10 9 8 7 6 5 4 3 2 1

Typeset by Pantek Arts, Maidstone, Kent
Printed and bound in Great Britain by Biddles Ltd, Guildford & King's Lynn

The Publishers' policy is to use paper manufactured from sustainable forests.

About the author

Debbie Harrison is an award-winning financial author and journalist. For her pensions and investment writing in 1998 alone she won the British Insurance and Investment Brokers Association Consumer Journalist of the Year and Technical News Journalist of the Year. She was also Scottish Life's Specialist Pensions Writer of the Year and the runner-up for two awards sponsored by Aon Consulting – Pensions and Investment Technical Journalist of the Year and Pensions and Investment Consumer Journalist of the Year. She is a regular contributor to the *Financial Times*, *Bloomberg Money*, *Investment Week* and *Employee Benefits*. Her previous consumer titles include *First Time Investor* and *Personal Financial Planner*, published by Financial Times Pitman Publishing. She also specialises in State and occupational pension scheme design and is the author of five *Financial Times* management reports on UK and international developments in these markets.

Contents

Preface

Today we should all invest for our retirement. For some this will mean a portfolio of direct equities but most people go into in the stockmarkets via collective pension funds – for example through an employer's pension scheme or through an individual plan which is based on life assurance funds or unit trusts. Given the plight of the welfare state, there is little doubt that the Government wants us to put aside even more to cover our financial needs in retirement. In future it may even force us to save a minimum percentage of our annual earnings.

While few would contest the importance of self-sufficiency, not everyone feels ready to proceed with confidence. Moreover, we often do not know to whom we can turn for help. Pensions jargon is formidable and for many years the State, employers and the companies that sell private pensions made very little effort to explain where your money was going and what precisely you would receive in terms of retirement benefits. They may even have misled or lied to pension scheme members.

So where do you start? The unfortunate fact is that if you do not understand an investment in the first place you are unlikely to be able to assess whether it offers good value for money or lives up to its promises. The history of financial fraud and pension mis-selling is littered with incomprehensible policies and plausible rogues. Which is why you should read on.

This book is designed to help you to help yourself. Despite all the adverse publicity there are many terrific company schemes and individual plans out there. This book will help you find them. *Pension Power* takes a robust, no-nonsense approach to the world of pensions and reduces to the level of common sense a process where jargon and obfuscation have for too long been employed in order to justify the remuneration of the incompetent and the unscrupulous.

Some readers will be keen to undertake their own research before they choose the right pension for their circumstances. In these pages you will find everything you need to get started, plus plenty of useful tips on how to select your retirement investments in the context of your overall financial planning.

Others will need more help. Higher earners, for example, may like the idea of running their own pension portfolio, but, due to business and family commitments, they simply do not have the time. It is a shame to invest large sums in a pension plan, only to see it struggle and fail due to hasty decisions and plain neglect. Those who can only afford a modest monthly pension contribution are equally at risk. Too many personal pensions incorporate such high charges that the annual return on small investments is virtually wiped out.

If you want someone else to help you select the right pension, you will need a financial adviser. The good news is that there are literally thousands of advisers out there eager to help you with your pension planning. The bad news is that it is not immediately obvious which are the experts and which have just made the switch into finance following a short career selling double glazing. *Pension Power* will show you how to identify the right type of advice for your needs and explains how to track down the best firm for your requirements. Choose well and you can delegate the job of selecting and monitoring your pension to an expert, leaving you free to do what you are good at, namely running your business, your family or both.

Whatever your investment needs, *Pension Power* may not turn you into an expert, but it will certainly help you to become wise before, rather than after the event.

Debbie Harrison

Acknowledgements

The author would like to thank Martin Korn and Martin Reynard, partners of the London firm of chartered accountants Blick Rothenberg, for providing invaluable technical advice throughout the preparation of this book.

Introduction

Over 11 million employees and their dependants in the UK rely on company pension schemes for their financial security in retirement and for important family protection insurances during their working lives. Over £750 billion is invested in occupational pension funds which are used to pay for these benefits. A further 5–6 million employees and self-employed have personal pensions which are invested in funds worth £225 billion. In addition, thousands of small businesses and professional partnerships operate pension schemes, which in some cases are unique to the UK.

But all pensions are not equal. For the same level of contributions, different schemes and plans will produce very different results. Company pension schemes offer benefits that range from the generous to the miserly. Some financial institutions sell individual plans that provide excellent results, while others offer an unholy combination of poor investment returns and excessive charges.

This book tells you how to spot the difference and where to go for unbiased advice.

YOUR MOST TAX-EFFICIENT INVESTMENT

Private pensions are arguably the most tax-efficient mainstream investment in the UK:

- you get full tax relief on your contributions;
- the fund rolls up virtually free of income and capital gains tax;
- the pension itself is taxed as income but you can take a substantial chunk of the fund at retirement as tax-free cash.

For the many people who do not belong to a company scheme that links the value of the pension to salary, the pension plan is simply a tax-efficient wrapper for your investments. In fact, apart from the rather anomalous tax-free cash lump sum, the whole system is based on tax deferral.

As an investment, there are four major factors that affect the fund at retirement:

- how much you pay in;
- how well your fund performs;
- how much is deducted by way of charges;
- the conversion rate when you exchange your fund at retirement for a regular guaranteed income.

It is important to remember that pension planning should not be tackled in isolation. A personal pension should be incorporated into your overall portfolio of investments (if you have one) in terms of asset allocation. A brief introduction to the fundamentals of investment is provided in Chapter 2.

At retirement you must use most of your pension fund to buy an annuity from an insurance company or friendly society. In return for your lump-sum investment, the company pays you an income guaranteed for life. The annuity 'rate' is the level of regular income your investment secures. Apart from the size of fund, this depends largely on the price of long-dated gilts. These are the investments insurance companies buy to generate the guaranteed income. Gilt prices fluctuate, so the timing of the annuity purchase is critical.

PENSION ADVISERS

By the time you retire, your pension is likely to be your most valuable asset after the family home. It might even be worth more than this – reason enough to seek expert advice on your choice of plan. In practice even the most seasoned investor will be daunted by the tax, contribution and benefit rules. So will many advisers. This is why good advice is essential – although it will not come free and neither is it that easy to find.

The UK is not short of advisers. In fact you could say it is rather over-blessed with the breed. Unfortunately the financial services regulators do not publish a list of 'jolly good' ones, so it's all down to legwork. This book describes the different categories of advisers and the addresses of organisations worth contacting to get you started in your search.

HOW THIS BOOK CAN HELP

The primary aim of *Pension Power* is to deepen understanding, to dispel fear and to put the control of pensions firmly in the grasp of those who pay for them. To do this it is important first to establish what you want from your scheme or plan; second to determine what help you really need to achieve your aims; and third to select the best possible arrangement in terms of performance, flexibility and cost.

Employees

For many employees membership of a company scheme is likely to represent the most valuable financial benefit after the salary itself. At least this is the case where the employer makes a substantial contribution and the trustees appoint and monitor competent professionals to run the fund. However, a small proportion of schemes offer very poor value for money. This book explains how employees can assess their scheme and, if necessary, top it up. It also explains the alternatives and who can help them if there is a problem.

The self-employed

Of the 25 million people in paid work in the UK, about 3.5 million are self-employed – a proportion that is growing rapidly as more and more employment is based on short-term contracts. Some of these self-employed have access to schemes that are run by groups of employers on an industry basis, rather than by a single company. If the Government's proposals for 'stakeholder' pensions go ahead we should see many more of these value-for-money group arrangements springing up. In the meantime the main option for the self-employed – and for employees without access to an occupational scheme – is an individual personal pension.

If you are not in a company or industry-wide scheme this book explains how to choose the best personal pension for your circumstances.

High earners and executives

While the average employee has little say in the choice of pension arrangement, senior executives often have considerable scope to influence their pension benefits and, if necessary, to establish an arrangement separate from or in addition to the main company scheme. The position of high earners becomes more complicated if their scope for making pension provision is restricted by the 'earnings cap', which limits to £90 600 (for the 1999–2000 tax year) the earnings on which contributions and, for company schemes, benefits can be based.

This book helps executives to identify the best combination of pension and other financial benefits. Higher earners also need to know the pros and cons of the various methods of topping up a 'capped' pension.

Professional partnerships

Professional partners, as Schedule D taxpayers, cannot belong to a company pension scheme even if they set one up for their staff. All too often they assume that their only option is an individual private plan. However, it is possible for partners to make substantial cost savings by pooling resources in a group self-invested personal pension (SIPP). In these pages you will find out how to control your investment decisions and, should you wish, to use the pension fund to help purchase new business premises.

Small businesses

Many small family businesses would like to establish a pension fund but feel that where cash is limited the business must take priority. Careful selection of the right small self-administered scheme (SSAS) can help directors to finance their retirement while simultaneously using the pension fund to develop their business. The options for directors of small businesses are examined in Chapter 13.

MISSION STATEMENT

Pension Power aims to clear the fog that surrounds pensions and to provide a lucid explanation of how and why schemes work the way they do. For many people, good-quality advice is essential. This book provides a guide to the role of advisers and explains how to select the right firm.

Pension Power does not offer a textbook approach to pensions law and practice. Instead, the author hopes that a clear appreciation of their pension needs will help employees, the self-employed, professional partnerships and small businesses successfully control one of their most valuable assets.

Index to lifecycle events

This special index can be used to locate the sections of this book that deal with pension planning for the major career and personal milestones in our lives. Note the pitfalls and check the tips ahead of time and you will place your financial security in retirement on a firm foundation.

1

How to choose your financial planner

- Which type of adviser?
- Qualifications
- Technology and research
- Paying for advice
- The client agreement

Summary

This chapter is aimed primarily at those who need to take pension matters into their own hands rather than members of occupational schemes. However, if after reading Chapter 7 on company pensions you feel you need to top up your benefits with a tax-efficient investment, then this chapter is also for you.

Individual pension arrangements and group schemes that do not link the pension to your salary generally are governed by the Financial Services Act (1986). The aim of the Act is to regulate the people responsible for selling investments rather than the products themselves. In the personal pensions market the Act has proved a resounding failure. Millions of people were mis-sold personal pensions in the late 1980s and early 1990s by salesmen and advisers who appeared to know everything about the size of sales commission on these plans, but nothing about their inherent unsuitability for employees with access to occupational schemes.

The thrust of the Government's new approach to investments is to regulate the products themselves to ensure low charges and flexible terms are offered. This regime in future will apply to stakeholder schemes and to individual savings accounts (ISAs), the main retail tax-efficient investment which replaced personal equity plans (PEPs) and tax-exempt special savings accounts (TESSAs) in April 1999.

However, many people will still require advice and this chapter is designed to point you in the right direction.

WHICH TYPE OF ADVISER?

Company representatives

As the name implies, company representatives (also known as direct salesmen and tied agents) are employed by – and work solely for – just one company. Their income usually comprises two elements – a basic salary and a commission element. Some representatives are remunerated purely by sales commission, which means if they don't sell you a policy they don't eat. Fortunately, over the past few years companies have moved away from this system and most pay reasonable basic salaries, so there is less need to verbally beat you into submission. Where commission is paid, the amount will depend on how much you agree to invest in a product and for how long.

Buying direct is not a bad thing. Some of the best pension products – as well as some of the worst – are sold in this way. Several notable newcomers to the pensions scene – including Virgin, Marks & Spencer and Tesco – sell direct and claim to offer good value for money as a result. The important point to remember is that direct sales advisers by law are only permitted to sell the products of the company they represent and through which they are authorised. So, if you are after a personal pension, you will not be told about the other 99 products available with their 99 different charging structures and 999 different fund links.

Buying direct, therefore, is worth considering if you are confident you know what to look for and can research the market thoroughly. But if you buy blind on the grounds that you like the record label, the underwear or the croissants, frankly, you are taking a gamble.

Appointed representatives

These are the companies which have a contract with a life office or other financial institution to sell one or more of its products in return for commission. The appointed representative is not necessarily employed or owned by the life office and may act independently in other lines of business.

A typical example of an appointed representative is a building society which offers an independent mortgage service but only sells the endowment and personal pension products of one life company (often its own). So, if you want an endowment mortgage you will borrow XYZ Building Society's money but there will be no choice of endowment products – you will have to take the ABC Life Assurance endowment, or lump it.

The appointed representative will tell you that the company is authorised to sell the endowment/pension products of just one company. Like the company representative, the appointed representative is not obliged to tell you how competitive that product is in terms of charges and performance.

Independent financial advisers

Independent financial advisers (IFAs) are not tied to one life assurance company. Their job is to examine your needs and to search the market for the product that offers the best value in terms of performance, charges and contract flexibility, among other factors. For this reason, in theory at least, you stand a better chance of coming away with the right pension plan than if you go to a company or appointed representative. However, the term 'independent' is not synonymous with 'expert'. IFAs vary considerably in their level of competence.

The term 'independent' is not synonymous with 'expert'.

Your choice of adviser will be dictated partly by your pocket and partly by your preferred investment route. If you are interested in a self-invested personal pension (*see* Chapter 5) and want to invest directly in equities as well as collective funds (unit trusts, investment trusts and insurance funds) then you will probably require the services of a stockbroker or investment manager. If you plan to invest purely in collective funds, what you need is a well-researched and experienced firm of independent financial advisers.

Use the contacts in Appendix 1 to draw up your shortlist of firms. Obviously, the cost of the advice is important and you should ask for a rough estimate before proceeding. There are three other important points you should consider:

- to what extent does the firm specialise in pensions?
- how well qualified are the staff?
- what research and technology does the firm use to help select the right plan?

The first question is straightforward. Ask the firm what proportion of its business is pensions related and how many people out of the total client base does it advise on pensions. If the answers are 'not a lot' and 'not many' respectively then the chances are you will find greater expertise elsewhere.

QUALIFICATIONS

Qualifications are becoming increasingly important in the financial services sector and are a good indication of a firm's commitment to high standards. Having said that, there are so many different qualifications – some of which are very basic indeed – that it is easy to get confused.

Stockbrokers are regulated by the Securities and Futures Authority (SFA). In order to give you advice they must first pass the SFA's 'Registered Person's Examinations'. A committed investment adviser is also likely to be a member of the Securities Institute. To become a full member, the adviser needs to pass the Institute's diploma, which is a professional-level qualification for practitioners who have already gained experience in such areas as securities, derivatives, corporate finance and investment management. Financial planners who have trained through the Institute of Financial Planning (IFP) generally demonstrate a high level of competence and independence. The Society of Financial Advisers (SOFA) also runs some tough examinations.

Apart from qualifications, a stockbroker should also be able to demonstrate quality of research and analysis. Larger firms will employ several UK companies analysts as this is the primary market for private client direct-equity investment. To supplement this research the firm probably will use Reuters for company news and the monthly *Estimate Directory*, which provides aggregate earnings and company forecasts for about 1300 UK companies. A second source of research is the market makers through which the stockbroker buys and sells shares. Daily research from the institutional heavyweights is good news – an on-line link is ideal. For more general investment advice you can go to a well-resourced and experienced firm of independent financial advisers or financial planners. This category includes an increasing number of chartered accountants and solicitors who specialise in financial planning.

By the end of June 1997 all advisers had to have a 'benchmark' or basic qualification. There are several of these but you are most likely to come across the Financial Planning Certificate (FPC). This is examined by the Chartered Insurance Institute (CII). The Securities Institute also runs a benchmark exam for independent advisers – the Investment Advice Certificate. Accountants and bankers have their own benchmark regulatory qualifications.

The next stage up from the FPC is the Advanced Financial Planning Certificate (AFPC), which includes a personal investment planning syllabus. The AFPC allows advisers to become full members of SOFA – the financial services arm of the CII. SOFA has launched associate and fellowship qualifications which it says ultimately will lead to chartered recognition for financial advisers on a par with other professionals. The AFPC also allows advisers to become associate members of the Institute of Financial Planning. Financial planning is a growing discipline which practitioners say provides an 'holistic' approach to independent financial advice – in other words, the planners consider all of your requirements including tax, life assurance, investment, pensions, school fees and legal aspects such as wills and trusts. The IFP also runs a fellowship exam and publishes a register of fellows for consumers (*see* Appendix 1).

TECHNOLOGY AND RESEARCH

Technology is no substitute for skill but it does help an adviser eliminate the companies that have a poor performance track record, high charges and inflexible contract conditions (for example exit penalties if you stop the plan early). For pension plans and life assurance products many firms of advisers use. The Research Department. Another good research resource for personal pensions is *Life and Pensions Review*, an on-line and paper-based service from actuaries and employee benefits consultants, Buck Consultants. This covers contract features in detail, but its primary focus is the investment process which Buck Consultants believe is the best indicator of good long-term future performance. Actuaries and employee benefits consultants Bacon & Woodrow also carry out a thorough survey of unit-linked personal pensions each year, while both Bacon & Woodrow and Watson Wyatt provide excellent annual surveys on additional voluntary contributions (*see* Chapter 8).

If you are interested in unit and investment trusts as part of your 'self-invested' pension portfolio (see Chapter 5), or you want a personal plan from one of these companies, one of the most respected sources of information for advisers is Standard & Poor (S&P) Fund Research, which provides performance ratings, explains how the performance was achieved and keeps track of fund managers. If a leading light defects to a rival investment company, S&P Fund Research swiftly re-rates all the relevant funds. Given the cost, you will not want to subscribe to the service yourself, but you can ask your adviser to check if your unit or investment trust has an 'A', 'AA' or 'AAA' S&P Fund Research rating. The extensive screening process analyses the quality of the investment group as a whole, as well as the individual manager and the team. Only the top 20 per cent out of the 1600 unit trusts available achieve even an 'A' rating.

The service also analyses discrete results and any reputable firm of investment advisers should do the same. Discrete results show year-on-year rather than cumulative performance. This is important because a good cumulative result over five years might mask an outstanding (possibly lucky) short-term performance followed by several years of mediocrity. Most published statistics are cumulative, so discrete results are difficult to analyse without access to a major statistics database such as Micropal or HSW Hindsight.

Technology and research aside, your adviser should be able to give a rational explanation of the firm's selection criteria. For a long-term pension plan it may be wise to stick to the large, well-established financial institutions which have a clear investment philosophy, plus substantial research and administrative resources. Ideally your plan should provide access to external fund managers rather than be limited to just one company.

Your adviser should be able to give a rational explanation of the firm's selection criteria.

PAYING FOR ADVICE

Advisers vary in the way they are remunerated. Some IFAs are remunerated entirely by commission paid by providers on the sale of products. Others – including the professional firms – are remunerated entirely by fees paid directly by clients. Yet others take part of the commission and a reduced fee for each sale. And then there are those who will operate on a commission or a fee basis depending on your preference: if you want to pay a fee, that's fine, but if you want to pay by commission, that's fine too. Helpful, perhaps. Confusing, certainly.

Commission rates vary depending on the size of premium and the term of the contract, so the more you plan to invest the more likely it is to be cost effective to pay a fee. Fee-based advisers charge anything from around £50–£250 per hour depending on whether you go to a local high-street adviser or a leading firm of consulting actuaries. As a rough guide however, for good pensions advice you can expect to pay at least £80–£130 per hour with an overall minimum total of about £300–£500 depending on the nature of the case and the seniority of the adviser.

It's easy to get bogged down in the commission v. fees debate and frankly not worth the time. The purists argue that if you want to make sure that your adviser is not influenced by the levels of commission available on different products, then the best route is the fee-based adviser. The pragmatists argue that for many people the level of fees charged by professionals is a deterrent. Whether you pay fees or commission the important point is to know what the total bill is likely to be and whether the commission structure makes your plan inflexible if you want to reduce or stop payments. In the past you had no chance of finding out because life and pension companies did not have to tell you, so in some cases got away with daylight robbery. However, since January 1995 companies have been required by the financial services regulators to disclose all their charges in full, including sales commission, in a pre-sale 'key features' document.

One of the particularly daft aspects of the tax system is that you pay fees out of your taxed income, on top of which you have to pay VAT. If you pay through the commission route, not only do you avoid VAT but effectively you get tax relief at your highest rate on the payment. This is because the commission is deducted from your pension contributions, which themselves benefit from full tax relief. Some providers of personal pensions have tried to get around this problem by designing a contract aimed at fee-based advisers that does not have an automatic allowance for commission payments built in. Under a 'nil commission' contract the adviser and client can agree a fee and ask the provider to deduct this from the first premium to avoid the VAT. If there is no product sale, the adviser can be paid a straight fee.

When you ask for the commission to be stripped out of your plan, make sure the pension company has not left in place the early surrender and transfer penalties associated with commission-based products. You should also ask what will happen to renewal commission (usually paid to the adviser from year two onwards) and incremental commission (a fresh chunk of commission paid on any increase in your contributions).

If you plan to pay pension contributions on a regular monthly basis you should take out 'waiver of premium' insurance. When you are too ill to work your pension company will continue to credit you with contributions up to your retirement date.

What if you change jobs

The Inland Revenue does not allow you to belong to a company pension scheme and to continue to run a personal pension. If you change jobs and join your new employer's scheme you must stop your personal pension contributions. In these circumstances, some personal pensions allow you to redirect your premiums into a free-standing additional voluntary contribution (FSAVC) plan which acts as a top-up to the company pension. This is a useful feature designed to avoid the financial penalties that might otherwise be charged when you stop payments to the personal pension.

However, if you negotiate the terms of your personal pension properly in the first place there should be no charges on early termination. FSAVCs are an excellent idea but should not be a condition of stopping payment to the personal pension plan. Besides, if you want to top up your company pension, your first choice should be your employer's in-house AVC scheme, since the running costs will be much lower for a group scheme compared with an individual plan where you have to bear the full brunt of all the charges. (For more details on topping up your company pension, *see* Chapter 8.)

Choice of low-cost personal pensions

'Low cost' in terms of personal pensions usually refers partly to the pension company's annual administration and fund management charges and partly to the level of commission deducted for the sale. Remember, if you do not pay commission you will have to pay your adviser a fee, so it is not a win–win situation.

There are several low or nil commission personal pensions, including the more sophisticated self-invested personal pensions (SIPPs) examined in Chapter 5. Other options include some of the unit and investment trust plans which tend to have a more flexible structure and impose an even charge on each contribution throughout the investment term. This is more flexible than the traditional life office plan which imposes most of the charges for the entire term up front. Over the long term there will be little difference in the two charging methods, but if you stop your plan in the early years the plan with heavy 'front-end' deductions will give you very little back.

There are two main company charges to consider. The 'initial' charge is usually about 5 per cent, although it can be higher if the adviser is paid a very large sales commission. The annual charge is typically 0.75 to 1 per cent of the value of your fund, although it can be as high as 1.5 per cent for a specialist fund or one that offers certain guarantees. The annual charge will have the greatest impact on your investment return over the long term.

Impact of charges on your fund

Your key features document will show what your fund might be worth at retirement assuming various rates of return (5 per cent, 7.5 per cent and 10 per cent). This is a bit of a pointless exercise since none of these rates is guaranteed and even if it were you would need to know what inflation rates applied during the investment period to get a feel for what your fund would be worth in real terms. However, the document should also show you the impact of charges on your fund at retirement and at earlier stages if you transfer to another company. This can be used to compare different companies' charges and flexibility.

One point to watch though. Low charges for one level of contribution does not indicate that charges are low across the board. Different charges apply to different premium levels and the effect of a flat-rate monthly policy fee, for example, will be proportionately greater on lower premiums.

THE CLIENT AGREEMENT

If you plan to use your adviser on a regular basis it is a good idea to have a written agreement which sets out the firm's terms and what services it will provide. A clearly worded client agreement gives you a benchmark against which you can judge the adviser's performance, particularly where the firm has direct responsibility for investing your money. For example, is the adviser monitoring the performance of your individual or small company pension

A clearly worded client agreement gives you a benchmark against which you can judge the adviser's performance.

plan and, if so, what action has been taken to offset any problems on charges and performance? Are you receiving regular updates on performance?

The following checklist includes the main points in a client agreement. You should add any further points that apply to your particular circumstances.

- The regulation of the adviser under the Financial Services Act 1986.
- Which services this entitles the adviser to carry out and the services it is not authorised to undertake. For example, is the adviser authorised to hold client money or custodial investments?
- Permission (required by the Consumer Credit Act 1974) for the adviser to act on your behalf to negotiate mortgages, loans and overdrafts.
- The period of agreement and period of notice on both sides (usually a minimum of 30 days).
- Your responsibility to provide the information the adviser needs (for example, the adviser needs a list of your existing investments and you need to be clear about your attitude to investment risk).
- The adviser's access to your other professional advisers, for example your bank manager, accountant and pension provider.
- Your right to veto any recommendations.
- A confidentiality clause.
- Details of how your documents will be stored.
- Fee rates per hour for different level of advisers within the firm and details of any due dates for regular fees.
- Details of VAT likely to be charged.
- Treatment of commissions if the adviser acts on a fee basis. Does the firm reinvest this money or offset it against fees?
- Treatment of complaints and disputes.

Key points

- The main factors that affect your annual return are performance and the cost of your investment, including the advice.
- Unless you are sure of your ability to research the market thoroughly, seek independent advice.
- Consider which type of firm is suitable – for example, do you need a stockbroker to advise on direct-equity investment or would you be happy with one of the firms of advisers that specialise in collective investments such as unit and investment trust plans?
- Check the level of qualifications held by the staff and the firm's research resources.
- Ideally, pay for your advice by fees rather than commission as this removes any potential bias in the firm's recommendations.

2

Equities and bonds without tears

- Risk
- Securities
- The main asset classes
- Risk and reward
- Spreading risk
- Different styles of institutional fund management
- Ethical pension investment

Summary

Savings and investment institutions are adept at dressing up what are essentially quite straightforward assets. As a result, it is easy to fall into the trap of investing in pensions without being aware of the underlying investments and how they fit in with your other savings. If you have more than one pension you could end up with the investment equivalent of a dog's dinner. What you need is a co-ordinated, well-balanced financial plan for retirement.

This chapter explains the characteristics of the asset classes you will come across in your quest for the best investments for your pension fund and other long-term savings. It will give you confidence to challenge advisers who try to blind you with science and baffle you with jargon. Go ahead and challenge them.

RISK

Crucial to your understanding of investments is your attitude to that four-letter word 'risk'. The technical definition of risk, in financial terms, is 'the standard deviation of the (arithmetic) average return'. It might be fun to discuss this with an overbearing adviser, but for most people the meaning of risk can be expressed more simply. The biggest perceived risk is the loss of your original capital. Equally important, however, is the loss of the real value of your capital through inflation.

Now, there is no such thing as a 'safe' investment or saving scheme but some are safer than others in terms of protecting your original capital. On the other hand, they may not protect you from inflation. The two chief dangers for private investors, therefore, are capital loss and inflation. These are discussed later in this chapter.

First it is helpful to look at the underlying asset classes in which you will invest.

SECURITIES

Investment literature uses a lot of confusing jargon. Commonly used (and misused) terms include 'securities', 'stocks' and 'shares'.

'Securities' is the general name for all stocks and shares. What we call 'shares' today were originally known as 'stocks' because they represented part ownership in the joint stock companies – the precursors to today's public limited companies or plcs. So, to some extent the terms stocks and shares are interchangeable, and we still use the terms stockmarkets and stockbrokers. Broadly speaking, stocks are fixed-interest securities and shares are the rest. The four main types of securities listed and traded on the UK Stock Exchange are:

- *UK ('domestic') equities* – ordinary shares issued by over 2000 UK companies;
- *Overseas equities* – ordinary shares issued by non-UK companies;

- *Bonds* – fixed-interest stocks issued by companies and local authorities, among others (think of them as a sophisticated type of IOU);
- *Gilts* – bonds issued by the UK Government to raise money to fund any shortfall in public expenditure.

THE MAIN ASSET CLASSES

If a company wants to raise finance it has two main options. It can sell part of the ownership of the company by issuing ordinary shares (equities) or it can borrow money by issuing bonds. All you need to create a market is organisations with something to sell and organisations which want to buy. Shares and bonds are bought and sold on the stockmarket.

UK equities

Equities are the quoted shares of companies in the UK and tend to dominate most pension funds, whether they are held directly or are pooled through collective funds such as unit trusts, open-ended investment companies, investment trusts or insurance funds.

A share or equity literally entitles the owner to a specified share in the profits of the company and, if the company is wound up, to a specified share of its assets. The owner of shares is entitled to the dividends – the six-monthly distribution to shareholders of part of the company's profits. The 'dividend yield' on equities is the dividend paid by a company divided by that company's share price. There is no set redemption date for an equity when the company is obliged to return your original investment. If, as a shareholder, you want to convert your investment into cash ('to realise its value') you must sell your shares.

Your aim is to invest in companies that will achieve a good return in exchange for an acceptable level of risk.

The return achieved by UK equities, when measured over the long term, has exceeded both price and earnings inflation. Your aim – or the aim of your investment manager – is to invest in companies that will achieve a good return for your money in exchange for an acceptable level of risk.

Overseas equities

These are similar in principle to UK equities but there are differences in shareholder rights. Investment overseas provides exposure to the growth in foreign markets including younger, fast-growing economies. However, these shares also expose you to different economic and political risks as well as currency fluctuations. This can be both good and bad, of course, but the point is that it adds an extra layer of risk.

As a rule of thumb, exposure to the major developed economies, for example the European Union countries, the US and Canada, is considered beneficial but generally is achieved through collective funds – for example investment trusts (*see* page 51). Exposure to the emerging economies is high risk and so only suitable for those prepared to take a punt.

Bonds

UK bonds are issued by borrowers. Where the borrower is the Government, these bonds are known as gilt-edged securities or just 'gilts'. Where the borrower is a company, the instruments are known as bonds or, more accurately, 'corporate bonds'. Bonds are also issued by local authorities, overseas governments and overseas companies.

In return for the loan of your money, the borrower agrees to pay a fixed rate of interest (known as the coupon) for the agreed period and to repay your original capital sum on a specified date, known as the maturity or redemption date.

The point to remember about fixed-interest securities is that the investment return is determined more by the level of interest rates than the issuing company's profitability (*see* below). Provided the issuer remains sufficiently secure to honour the future coupon payments (the regular interest) and redemption payment (the return of the original capital) you know exactly what your return will be, provided you hold the bond to maturity. Gilts offer the highest degree of security because they are issued by the UK Government.

If you or a fund manager sells a bond before its maturity date, then the value of the future coupon and redemption payments will depend on the prevailing interest rates at the time of sale. So, if interest rates are rising, then the value of the fixed-interest security will fall. This is because for the same amount of capital invested, you could get a better return elsewhere. Conversely, if interest rates are falling, then the value of the fixed-interest security will be higher because it provides a greater stream of income than you could get from alternative sources.

This volatile pattern of behaviour is more apparent with fixed-interest securities which have a long period to run to maturity, since they are more likely to be traded before redemption date.

To summarise, as a general rule equities are considered more risky and volatile than bonds because they behave in an unpredictable way whereas, provided the company or Government backing a bond is watertight, the return on a bond held to maturity is predictable. However, it is not predictable if you decide to sell before maturity.

■ Index-linked gilts

Index-linked gilts are issued by the UK Government and are guaranteed to provide interest payments (the coupon) and a redemption value that increase in line with annual inflation. For this reason they are one of the lowest risk assets for income seekers, although they may not necessarily provide a competitive return.

■ Cash

'Cash' does not mean stacks of £20 notes stuffed under the mattress but usually refers to money on deposit. Deposits have the advantage that the value in monetary terms is known and is certain at all times. What is unknown is the interest that will be received and by how much this may fall short of the rate of inflation.

Property

In investment terms, 'property' usually refers to the ownership of land and buildings that are used by a business or other organisation. The owner of the property receives income from the rent charged to the tenant and, over time, this rent is expected broadly to keep pace with inflation. The dominant factor in the value of a property is the desirability or otherwise of its location.

There are several problems with property. First, it is often sold in large blocks that cannot be easily split for investment purposes. As a result, only the larger institutional funds can afford (or are wise) to own property directly. Second, property is a very illiquid asset and it can take several years for the right selling conditions to arise.

RISK AND REWARD

When you take a risk – for example by investing in equities rather than putting your money on deposit – you expect a commensurate reward. The reward for investors is the total return, which is usually expressed as a percentage increase of the original investment. This may be a combination of income (or yield) plus capital growth (or rise in the market price). Risk is very subjective. Like beauty, it is in the eye of the beholder. To help you gauge your attitude to risk it is helpful to consider the twin evils mentioned above.

Inflation risk

Savings and investments which expose you to inflation risk usually fall into the 'safe' category. For example, we all tend to think of bank and building society deposit accounts as risk free. But are they ? If you are worried about the risk of losing your original capital then, provided you stick to the well-regulated UK building societies and banks, you can put your money on deposit and your original capital will be safe. Your capital will not diminish, indeed it will grow, assuming income is reinvested. However, the growth will be modest and in real (that is, inflation-adjusted) terms, it may not always match the rate of inflation.

This does not mean you should ignore deposit accounts. In practice they play a very important part in pension planning – particularly in the run-up to retirement when you may want to consolidate your gains and protect your capital by moving into a combination of cash (deposits) and gilts.

Bonds can offer the prospect of higher returns than a deposit account but they do not offer any guaranteed protection against increases in inflation.

Capital risk

Historically, if you wanted to match or beat inflation over the long term you would have had to invest in equities, although in recent years the gap between bonds and equities has narrowed. With equities, unless your fund offers a guarantee (and these can be costly – *see* page 55), your capital certainly is at risk. So, when you see the statutory wealth warning that your investment can go down as well as up, take it seriously.

SPREADING RISK

Risk can be managed in different ways. You can concentrate it in a single investment or spread it over a wide range. For example, if you invest all your money in a single share and it does well you will be in clover. If the company goes bust you could lose the lot.

It is wise to spread risk by investing in a range of shares either directly or through collective funds such as unit and investment trusts. Note, however, that even with collective funds the risk rating varies considerably. At one end of the spectrum are the higher risk specialist funds which tend to be small and managed on an aggressive basis. At the other, more comfortable end, are the large UK equity or international funds which offer greater immunity to the capricious behaviour of stockmarkets. Bear in mind, though, that even the most broadly diversified funds will be hit when stockmarkets crash.

Even the most broadly diversified funds will be hit when stockmarkets crash.

You can protect yourself further from risk if you diversify into different asset classes – for example, instead of just investing in UK equities, you could include some overseas equities, bonds, gilts, deposits and, possibly, property in your portfolio. Each asset class behaves in a different way and therefore a careful asset allocation will protect you from swings in the economic cycle. Institutional pension funds invest across all the main asset classes, although the biggest proportion is in UK equities.

Inflation

It is also important to keep in mind the relationship between inflation and returns. At the time of writing the Government's aim was to keep inflation under 2.5 per cent. This is based on a definition of retail price inflation that excludes mortgage interest payments.

Inflation is a key determinant of the real investment return. Stockmarkets may not be prepared for a sudden rise or fall in inflation but they tend to adjust over time and provide a long-term hedge against price rises. Gilts and cash are not considered suitable as a long-term hedge against inflation.

Period of investment

Clearly, long-term returns on equities, gilts and cash should be viewed with some caution and certainly should not be treated as a guide to the future. While history indicates that equities should provide a better return than bonds over the medium to long term, there is an important caveat.

'Medium' term means a minimum of five years. Long term is more like 10–15 years. If you go into the stockmarkets for shorter periods you are in danger of getting your fingers burned, either because the markets take a tumble just before you want to get out or because the fixed costs associated with buying your investments undermine the return over the short term.

How your pension fund is run

It is rarely wise for a private investor to imitate the style of an institutional fund manager but it is interesting to watch how they behave. The large pension funds, for example, are worth millions of pounds. Some run into billions. This means they can make money on minor price changes due to the sheer volume of their transactions. Moreover, compared with an individual investor, institutional funds benefit from very low dealing costs. This means that what might trigger a buy or sell transaction in the institutional market often should be interpreted as a much more cautious 'hold' position by the private investor.

DIFFERENT STYLES OF INSTITUTIONAL FUND MANAGEMENT

Asset management has its own language and it is helpful to understand the tactical and strategic techniques employed on your behalf. Never be afraid to ask questions and remember that one of the chief characteristics of stockbrokers and fund management groups is a high ratio of ego to square footage of office space. It is not always backed by genuine intelligence, common sense and honesty, as the frequent investment scandals demonstrate.

The following descriptions are a broad guide to help you bluff your way through the initial meetings.

Active managers

Active investment managers aim to increase a fund's value by deviating from a specific benchmark – for example a stockmarket index. There are two basic techniques used in active stock selection.

The starting point for active managers who adopt a 'bottom up' approach is the company in which the manager may invest. The manager will look at in-house and external research on the company's history and potential future prospects. This will include an examination of the strength of the balance sheet, the company's trading history, the management's business strategy and the price/earnings ratio (the market price of a share divided by the company's earnings/profits per share in its latest 12-month trading period). From the company analysis the manager will proceed to look at the general performance and prospects for that sector (for example construction, food retailers and so on) and then take into consideration national and international economic factors.

The 'top down' manager works in reverse, looking first at the international and national economic factors that might affect economic growth in a country, geographic area (for example the 'Tiger' economies of South-east Asia) or economic category (emerging markets, for example) and gradually work down to the individual companies.

Active managers also have a style. For example 'value' managers seek out under-researched companies with potential. Some of the biggest names in institutional pension fund management have underperformed in recent years, partly because managers with this philosophy tend to avoid the biggest FTSE (Financial Times – Stock Exchange) 100 companies if they appear overpriced – yet this is where the main market growth has occurred.

Passive managers

Passive managers aim to track or replicate a benchmark. This style is also known as index tracking. It may sound simple but in practice this is a complex process based on emulating the performance of a particular stockmarket index by buying all or a wide sample of the constituent shares. The passive manager does not consider the merits of each stock (of different sectors and of economic cycles). If it is in the index then it must be represented in the fund. To date, index tracking funds have done very well compared with actively managed funds, largely because the passive manager's charges are very low.

Passive management becomes very complicated when the process tries to outstrip the index returns by deviating in a specific way. This is known as quantitative management. Frankly, if you are interested in this subject you should be reading a different book. Suffice it to say that if you ever meet a quant manager at a dinner party, introduce them to the derivatives specialist and make your exit.

ETHICAL PENSION INVESTMENT

Ask ten people what they think is ethical and you will get ten different answers. Ethical views, by their very nature, are subjective.

An ethical pension fund should not be expected to reflect market movements as a whole.

If you have strong ethical views you must consider several issues carefully before you try to apply them to your pension fund. First, you need to translate your views into a clear mandate, and second, you need to appreciate the impact any ethical screening process will have on a fund's annual returns. An ethical pension fund must have an appropriate performance benchmark and should not be expected to reflect market movements as a whole.

The cost of research

Ethical investment is a complicated subject and is not helped by the difficulty and cost of obtaining sufficient data upon which to form a view about the business of 'ethical' companies. A good source of information for people interested in this subject is the Ethical Investment Research Service (EIRIS) which maintains a database of ethical funds and individual companies. EIRIS can provide a list of pension companies which offer ethical funds, but it is important to note that many of the top names in pensions are not on this list.

Defining an ethical policy

The major exclusions in ethical funds tend to be arms, alcohol, tobacco, gambling, animal testing, environmental damage and the payment of exploitative wages in developing countries. But the list could extend almost indefinitely. Some funds take a proactive approach and aim to invest in companies which are working towards a desirable goal – 'green' companies involved in recycling or environmentally friendly waste disposal, for example. Environmental funds can also be regarded as ethical. Here the choice of shares will depend on a company's environmental policy in terms of pollution, ozone depletion, deforestation and waste management, among other criteria.

If you have strong ethical views you need to decide where to draw the line. It is one thing to exclude tobacco and/or alcohol companies, but what about the supermarkets which sell their products? Gambling is also a typical exclusion, but does this mean all the outlets that sell tickets for the National Lottery should be avoided? Some ethical investors might favour pharmaceutical companies because of their groundbreaking research in the wars against cancer and AIDS, for example. Others might exclude the same companies on the grounds that they carry out experiments on animals.

The impact of ethical screening on performance

Critics of ethical investment argue that performance suffers due to the exclusion of many major FTSE 100 companies, most of which have something distinctly unethical somewhere among their diverse operations. If a fund excludes the very obvious unethical villains, shown in Table 2.1, it would lose access to about 8 per cent of the stockmarket by value. This figure grows if you add animal testing, nuclear power, and environmental damage, for example. The full EIRIS screening, shown in Table 2.2, disqualifies up to 60 per cent of the FTSE 100 companies.

This means that an ethical pension fund is likely to have a disproportionate weighting towards smaller, more risky companies. As far as performance goes, smaller companies have the ability to outperform their larger counterparts, but they are inclined to be more volatile and must be selected with great care, as the performance of the FTSE 250 and SmallCap (the smallest 550 or so in the FTSE All-Share Index) have demonstrated over the past few years. Also bear in mind that when the SmallCap does well it is often due to the stunning outperformance of a handful of companies rather than a consistently good performance across the board.

In addition, there is a danger that the ethical policy leaves a fund over-exposed to certain sectors that may only be ethical by default – the hotels and leisure industry, for example. Moreover, the fund would be unable to reap the rewards of a boom in other sectors such as chemicals, engineering or pharmaceuticals.

A good year to examine in this context is 1997, when most general ethical funds underperformed the market as a whole because they had limited exposure to the sectors that did well. Typical exclusions that proved regrettable from the performance point of view included banks (most lend money indiscriminately to non-ethical companies and countries with poor human rights records), integrated oils (environmental damage) and pharmaceuticals (animal testing and, occasionally, exploitation in tests on humans in emerging countries).

Table 2.1 Large companies commonly avoided by ethical investors

Company	*Stockmarket weighting %*	*Arms*	*Alcohol*	*Tobacco*	*Gambling*
Allied Domecq	0.43		*		
Bass	0.52		*		*
BAT	0.62			*	
Bowthorpe	0.05	*			
British Aerospace	0.67	*			
Cobham	0.05	*			
Diageo	1.84		*	*	*
Gallaher	0.21			*	
GEC	1.09	*			
GKN	0.42	*			
Greenalls	0.07		*		
Greene King	0.02		*		
Highland Distillers	0.03		*	*	
Imperial Tobacco	0.25			*	
Ladbroke	0.22				*
Racal	0.08	*			
Rank	0.13				
Rolls-Royce	0.28	*			
Scottish & Newcastle	0.32		*		
Smiths Industries	0.20	*			
TI	0.12	*			
Tomkins	0.25	*			
Vaux	0.03				
Vickers	0.03	*			
Wetherspoon	0.03		*		
Whitbread	0.28		*		
Total % FTSE	8.24				

Source: Chiswell Associates

Table 2.2 Just how far do you go?

EIRIS researches over 1000 companies. The screening options from which you can choose include:
■ alcohol ■ animals (meat production and sale, leather/fur manufacture and sale) ■ arms and sales to military purchasers ■ community involvement ■ corporate governance ■ directors' pay ■ environmental issues ■ equal opportunities ■ gambling ■ greenhouse gases ■ health and safety convictions ■ human rights ■ intensive farming ■ military contracts ■ newspaper production and television ■ nuclear power (fuel, components and construction of plants) ■ overseas interests (wages exploitation in emerging economies, deriving profits from countries with poor human rights records) ■ ozone-depleting chemicals ■ pesticides ■ political contributions ■ pornography ■ Third World involvement ■ tobacco ■ tropical hardwood ■ waste disposal ■ water pollution

Source: EIRIS

Key points

- 'Securities' refers to UK equities, overseas equities, gilts and bonds.
- If a company wants to raise finance, it can issue shares, which represent a share in the ownership, or bonds, which are a form of debt and behave like a sophisticated IOU.
- If you want to match or beat inflation, historically you would have had to invest in equities.
- Inflation has a major impact on the real return provided by your investments.
- Equities are only suitable for the medium to long term, due to their volatility and the cost of investing.
- Ethical pension funds tend to concentrate on smaller, more risky companies, so the performance can be more volatile.

Further information

EIRIS *Money & Ethics*, a guide to collective funds, is available from EIRIS, price £15. Also available free from EIRIS are a guide to financial advisers who offer advice on ethical investments and a guide to fund managers and stockbrokers who manage portfolios with ethical constraints. Contact EIRIS, 504 Bondway Business Centre, 71 Bondway, London SW8 1SQ.

Life and Pensions Moneyfacts lists ethical and environmental life assurance and pension funds plus unit trusts. Contact Moneyfacts, Moneyfacts House, 66–70 Thorpe Road, Norwich NR1 1BJ.
Tel: 01603 476476.

3

Personal pensions

- Background
- Choosing a personal pension
- How they work
- Appropriate personal pensions
- Standard personal pensions
- Retirement annuity plans
- Choice of personal pension plan
- Group personal pensions
- Special uses for personal pensions

Summary

To date, personal pensions have been the main option for the self-employed and for employees who do not have access to a company pension scheme. Unfortunately in the late 1980s and early 1990s these plans were mis-sold to such an extent that the Government has been forced to take drastic action to restore the consumer's faith in private individual pensions. Its chief aim is to make available more group schemes organised on an industry, rather than single employer basis. Industry-wide and stakeholder pension schemes are discussed on page 79. However, this will still leave many people – particularly the self-employed – without access to a group scheme and the economies of scale they confer. For these people the Government intends to encourage pension providers to offer simpler, cheaper and more flexible personal pensions than have been widely available in the past.

There is nothing new in these aims. Neither is there anything wrong with the concept of personal pensions. First-class providers have always combined a good choice of asset managers and flexibility with competitive charges. In the previous Conservative Government's eagerness to get people out of the State scheme, it failed to vet providers properly. Providers and advisers got away with blue murder due to the Government's neglect and ignorance.

This chapter explains how to get maximum flexibility and value for money. It also looks at performance – the one major aspect of personal pensions that the Government cannot control. Without good performance all your hard work in selecting a pension plan will come to nothing. There is little comfort in knowing that you have had a flexible contract with low charges if, at retirement, the performance has been so poor your fund will not secure you a decent income.

BACKGROUND

Personal pensions were launched in July 1988 as part of a Government campaign to extend individual pension choice. These plans replaced the old self-employed retirement annuities and in addition had two new features. First, they could accept employer contributions and, second, they allowed employees to contract out of the State Earnings-Related Pension Scheme (SERPS) on an individual basis and in return receive a rebate of National Insurance contributions (NICs) to invest in a plan of their choice. Previously this was only possible through membership of an occupational scheme that was contracted out of SERPS on a group basis. (Employees who are not members of a contracted-out group scheme are automatically in SERPS.)

As discussed in Chapter 16, over the next few years the value of SERPS will be cut and ultimately this scheme will be replaced by the new flat-rate State Second Pension, which will only be open to very low earners. Everyone else will have to make private provision.

It is extremely unwise to rely solely on your SERPS benefits, or on the pension derived from investing the rebate of NI contributions, to provide an adequate income in retirement.

CHOOSING A PERSONAL PENSION

Before you buy a personal pension it is helpful to understand how these products work. For advice on how to pay for your plan and the impact this has on charges and flexibility, *see* Chapter 1.

Personal pensions do not provide a pension linked to salary. Instead the plans operate on a 'money purchase' or 'defined contribution' basis which means that your contributions are invested to build up a fund that is used at retirement to buy an annuity. The level of guaranteed regular income you secure will depend on the fund size – and therefore performance – and how much the provider has deducted in charges, among other factors. It will also depend on annuity rates – that is, the amount of regular income your fund will secure at retirement.

The main criteria on which your choice of personal pension should be based include:

- the performance track record, with the emphasis on consistently competitive annual returns over the long term;
- preferably access to a range of investment managers;
- the flexibility of the contract – for example, there should be no financial penalties for reducing and stopping contributions, transferring the fund and early retirement;
- the financial strength of the provider;
- the level of charges deducted during the lifetime of the policy;
- the cost of advice.

HOW THEY WORK

There are two component parts of a personal pension, although for the sake of convenience providers tend to lump these together. The 'appropriate' personal pension is used to contract out of SERPS, while a 'top-up' personal pension is used to take extra contributions in addition to the contracted-out rebate.

Like all pension arrangements approved by the Inland Revenue, the personal plan is a tax-efficient way of saving for retirement:

- contributions qualify for full tax relief;
- the pension fund grows virtually free of tax;
- up to 25 per cent of the main pension fund at retirement can be taken as tax-free cash.

The rest of the fund (75 per cent) must be used to purchase an annuity to provide the retirement income. The annuity can be bought at any age between 50 and 75. The annuity is taxed as earned income, so your annual income tax allowance can still be used (*see* Chapter 6).

The personal plan is a tax-efficient way of saving for retirement.

Almost anyone over age 16 can take out a personal pension provided he or she has an earned income.

APPROPRIATE PERSONAL PENSIONS

If you want to opt out of SERPS you need an appropriate personal pension. These plans are designed primarily for two categories of employees:

- employees who do not have access to an occupational scheme;
- employees whose company scheme is 'contracted in' to SERPS where the scheme benefits are paid in addition to the SERPS pension.

The self-employed do not pay in to SERPS and so cannot take out an appropriate personal pension.

These factors must be considered in conjunction with an important caveat: if you earn less than £12 000 a year, under normal circumstances you should not opt out of SERPS using an appropriate personal pension. On these earnings your rebate is worth about £350–£400 a year and you will find that most providers' charges will render this level of contribution uneconomic unless you also save through a standard personal pension (*see* page 39).

Opinion varies on who should contract out of SERPS. Some advisers argue that women should not consider this option at all, and that only men up to age 50 may benefit. However, there are other issues to consider – for example, you may prefer to have control of your own pension rather than rely on the Government to look after it for you. You should also take into consideration the fact that previous governments have reduced the benefits of SERPS, so the guarantees offered by this State scheme are not as rock solid as they might appear.

How the rebate works

Nevertheless, the main reason for opting out is to achieve a better pension by investing the rebate. Unfortunately, this is one of those apples and pears comparisons, which is why you get so many different opinions on who should opt out and at what age/level of earnings. SERPS, like final salary company schemes, offers a guaranteed benefit linked to earnings (that is, guaranteed until the

Government changes the rules again), whereas the pension you receive from a personal plan depends on investment returns, charges and annuity rates at the time of retirement.

In order to decide whether you should contract out, an adviser or pension company has to assume a certain rate of return for your investment, a certain level of charges in the plan and a certain annuity rate. However confident your adviser appears, this calculation involves a great deal of guesswork.

If you do contract out of SERPS, your adviser should review this decision each year.

How the NI rebate is calculated

The rebate is calculated as a percentage of an employee's 'band earnings' – that is, earnings between the lower and upper threshold for NI contributions. For the 1999–2000 tax year the NI thresholds are £66 per week (£3432 per annum) and £500 per week (£26 000 per annum), giving annual 'band earnings' of £22 568. The rebate ranges from just over 3 per cent to 9 per cent of band earnings, depending on age. So, the rebate for those earning £26 000 or over would range from about £770 for young employees to about £2030 at age 46 and over.

The rebate is sent by the Department of Social Security (DSS) direct to your personal pension provider after the end of the tax year to which the rebate relates. It is always worth checking that your provider receives this promptly since a delay in investment will reduce the returns. At the time of writing the DSS was experiencing severe delays in payments of NI rebates due to problems with the new National Insurance Recording System computer. However, it will automatically include compensation when it finally does make the payments.

Pension provided by the rebate fund

The fund built up from the NI rebates is known as 'protected rights'. In fact the description 'protected' is somewhat anomalous since the fund's value is not guaranteed in any way. The rules on protected rights funds are complicated (no surprise here) but are broadly as follows:

- the fund cannot be used to provide tax-free cash;
- the annuity purchased with the fund must provide for a spouse's pension, worth 50 per cent of the personal pension planholder's pension;
- the annuity payments must be increased each year by the rate of inflation (or 5 per cent – whichever is the lower figure).

These are valuable features but, as is explained in Chapter 6, extra protection features for annuities carry a cost and therefore reduce the level of the income you secure with your fund.

STANDARD PERSONAL PENSIONS

In addition to the NI rebate, you can and should contribute a significant proportion of your earnings into a personal pension. Employees base their contributions on what the Inland Revenue calls 'net relevant earnings', which are roughly equivalent to annual earnings from any self-employed activities (after deducting losses and certain business charges on income) or from employment where you are not in a company pension scheme.

The annual contribution limits are given in Table 3.1 (but *see* 'High earners' on page 41).

Table 3.1 Maximum annual contributions to a personal pension

Age	*% net relevant earnings*
Up to 35	17.5 per cent
36–45	20 per cent
46–50	25 per cent
51–55	30 per cent
56–60	35 per cent
61–74	40 per cent

Notes: The maximum annual contributions relate to the tax year and so will depend on your age on 6 April. All personal pension contributions are subject to the earnings cap, which limits the amount of salary that can be used for pension purposes to £90 600 for the 1999–2000 tax year.

The amount you save must take into consideration the amount you already have in your fund.

It is possible to run more than one top-up personal pension plan provided total contributions fall within these limits. However, an employee can only have one appropriate plan for each tax year.

Your adviser should be able to help you assess the right contribution level. Table 3.2, with figures provided by the Office of Fair Trading (OFT), shows how much you should pay in if you want to have a pension comparable to the maximum possible under a company final salary scheme – that is, two-thirds of your final salary. It looks rather complicated but is designed to make a very important point, namely that the amount you save must take into consideration the amount you already have in your fund. You can also take account of any other sources of income in retirement.

Table 3.2 Your annual contribution depends on what you have already saved

Current size of fund as a % your salary	*Annual contribution (%) at the age you start your pension plan*				
	25	*30*	*40*	*50*	*60*
0	10	13	23	46	74
100	5	8	18	38	63
200	0	3	12	30	52
300	0	0	6	22	41
400	0	0	0	14	30

Notes: The figures represent the annual contributions recommended, expressed as a percentage of earnings. They assume the following: a retirement age of 65, a targeted pension of two-thirds final salary, a real rate of return of 8 per cent and annual expenses of 0.5 per cent. They also assume that the Inland Revenue maximum contribution limits are scrapped.

Employer's contributions

Employers can contribute to an individual employee's plan, although there is no legal requirement for them to do so. Total contributions must stay within the maximum percentages shown in Table 3.1.

High earners

High earners with personal pensions are restricted by the 'earnings cap', introduced in the 1989 budget, which limits the amount of salary that can be taken into consideration for contributions. For the 1999–2000 tax year the cap is £90 600 which means that the maximum contribution for an employee aged under 35 is 17.5 per cent of the cap – £15 855. In practice, it is hard to see how this would act as a restriction for younger people who tend to be financially stretched by family commitments and mortgage repayments. Older employees, however, often need to pay higher contributions if they have made little provision earlier in life.

Making extra large contributions

A special provision exists for employees and the self-employed who have not used up all their tax relief in previous years. Under the Inland Revenue's 'carry back' and 'carry forward' rules it is possible to 'mop up' unused relief for up to seven previous tax years. This is a very tax-efficient but complex exercise and should be discussed with your accountant or a pensions adviser with tax expertise.

Life assurance

It is also possible to use up to 5 per cent of the contribution limit to pay for life assurance, which effectively gives you tax relief on the premiums. Life assurance rates vary considerably, so you should shop around. If your pension provider's terms are expensive it might be cheaper to buy it elsewhere.

Insuring against illness

It is important to protect your pension if you become too ill to work and can no longer pay the contributions. 'Waiver of contribution' insurance does just that and is vital. If you can no longer work, the pension company credits your fund with the contributions between the date your earnings stop and your retirement age.

RETIREMENT ANNUITY PLANS

Many people still have a retirement annuity plan (RAP) – the predecessor to the personal pension. After July 1988 sales of these contracts stopped but existing policyholders can continue to contribute to existing plans. RAP contribution limits are lower in terms of percentages than for personal pensions, but these older plans are not subject to the earnings cap. The annual limits are shown in Table 3.3.

Table 3.3 Retirement annuity plans: maximum annual contributions

Age	*% net relevant earnings*
Up to age 50	17.5
51–55	20
56–60	22.5
61–74	27.5

Depending on your age at retirement and the prevailing annuity rates, it may be possible to take more than 25 per cent of the retirement annuity fund as tax-free cash since the calculation is not a straight percentage of the fund. The other main differences between the two arrangements is that you cannot contract out of SERPS with one of these older contracts, and your employer cannot contribute.

If you have one of the earlier plans it is worth checking the death-before-retirement benefits, since some of the early contracts offered very meagre returns – for example a return of contributions but without interest. At the same time make sure your old-style contract is written under trust. Some of the earlier retirement annuities did not do so automatically and this could lead to an inheritance tax problem for your dependants when you die.

Provided you are happy with the investment performance of your retirement annuity contract, your expected level of contribution fits in comfortably with the annual limits and you have satisfied yourself that the charges are competitive, there is no need to change to a personal pension. However, if you want to spread risk

If you want to spread risk between different providers and run a personal pension then you should seek professional independent advice.

between different providers and run a personal pension as well, then you should seek professional independent advice to determine the best way to achieve this. It is possible to contribute to both types of plans, but you have to take care to keep within the Revenue's maximum contribution rules.

CHOICE OF PERSONAL PENSION PLAN

Personal pensions are available from dozens of financial institutions, but the market is dominated by the life offices. An increasing number of unit trust and investment trust groups also offer their own personal pensions, as do some of the major institutional fund managers. Most banks and building societies tend to sell the plans run by their own life office. The next chapter will look at the important issues of fund choice and charges.

GROUP PERSONAL PENSIONS

Group personal pensions are becoming very popular, particularly among companies that do not want the expense and administrative burden of running a final salary pension scheme. The life offices also dominate this market, but an increasing number of institutional pension fund managers are joining the fray.

If your employer offers a group personal pension, see the section on group money purchase schemes which starts on page 89. This will help you decide whether the terms are flexible and the asset management is a good standard. In particular you should check the amount your employer is prepared to pay on your behalf and whether there are any penalties if you reduce or stop your own contributions when you change jobs.

At their most basic, group personal pensions are no more than a collection of individual plans. However, the more sophisticated schemes, usually negotiated by a consultant, make full use of the potential for economies of scale to reduce administration and investment charges. More generous plans feature employer contributions, free death benefits and free or low-cost disability insurance. Whether your group plan is generous or not will depend on how much your employer is prepared to pay.

Ideally your employer will arrange the group personal pension on a 'nil commission' basis. This means that the commission costs are stripped out and your employer's adviser is paid a fee. The main advantage of this system is a clear, flexible charging structure – you can see exactly what you are paying and if you change the amount of contribution or stop paying altogether there is no penalty. With any luck your employer may cover the charges and not pass them on to scheme members.

SPECIAL USES FOR PERSONAL PENSIONS

There are several unusual employment situations where a personal pension is useful.

Stop gap

Some company schemes have a high entry age, usually around 30. This is common among companies that have a rapid turnover of younger staff and do not want the administration hassle of refunding contributions or arranging transfer values. Younger employees can use a personal pension as a stop gap between the date of joining the company and the date of becoming eligible to join the pension scheme. Contributions to personal pensions during the waiting period must stop when the employee joins the company scheme, so it is essential to avoid locking yourself in to a regular premium plan that imposes early termination penalties.

Ineligible to join company scheme

Contract workers, part-timers and those with very low earnings may find that they are ineligible to join the company pension scheme, in which case a personal pension is the best alternative.

Limited benefits under company scheme

Occasionally an occupational scheme may be established to provide only death and dependants' benefits. In these cases it is possible to take out a personal pension.

Company scheme contracted in to SERPS

Some company schemes do not contract the membership out of SERPS. If you want to contract out on an individual basis you can use an appropriate personal pension and still remain in the company scheme.

Freelance earnings

Employees in a company scheme who have earnings from a second source – freelance work for example – can also take out a personal pension with contributions based on those earnings.

Transfers

Finally, personal pension plans can be used to accept a transfer value from a preserved company pension or from another individual pension plan. This is a complex area and the subject of considerable controversy since the mass mis-selling of plans for this purpose in the late 1980s. (*See* Chapter 10 for advice on transfers.)

Personal pension mortgages

It is possible to arrange to pay off your interest-only mortgage through a personal pension plan, making use of the tax-free cash on retirement to repay the outstanding capital. This may be worth considering if you do not already pay maximum contributions to your pension plan. However, the first consideration must be to ensure an adequate retirement income, so it may be better to use an individual savings account (ISA), for example, rather than your pension plan for this purpose.

Key points

Don't:

- Consider opting out of SERPS with an 'appropriate' personal pension if you earn less than £12 000 a year.
- Rely on the investment of the National Insurance rebate to provide you with a good pension. You will need to top up with extra contributions.
- Buy a personal pension if you have access to a good company pension scheme. Company pensions generally represent better value for money and usually provide good death and disability benefits as well.

Do:

- Seek help from an independent financial adviser (*see* Chapter 1).
- Check the past performance results thoroughly (ask to see the independent surveys and not the provider's interpretations of these results).
- Seek advice on the choice of fund. Younger people should invest more in equities but older people usually gradually switch to safer investments such as gilts.
- Check the flexibility of the plan. You should be able to reduce or stop contributions or transfer to another provider without penalty.
- Pay a sensible amount into your personal pension plan if this will be your main source of retirement income (*see* page 40).
- Try to get your employer to contribute. This is something to ask your new employer if you are about to change jobs.
- Boost your life assurance through your personal pension if appropriate, since you will get tax relief on the premiums. Shop around first though – in some cases the personal pension provider might charge high rates for term assurance and it may be cheaper to get it elsewhere, even without the tax relief.

4

How to find competitive performance and charges

- The underlying assets
- Unit-linked funds
- Unit trust funds
- Investment trust plans
- With-profits funds
- Unitised with-profits funds
- The new with-profits funds
- Guaranteed equity funds
- Lifestyle funds
- Self-invested personal pensions

Summary

The two most obvious factors that will affect the value of your pension fund at retirement are performance and charges. What you need is a combination of good long-term performance and competitive charges. If you are not careful, what you will end up with is high charges and mediocre performance, which will result in very poor returns for your contributions. Cheap is not necessarily cheerful, so don't buy on the basis of low cost alone. Some of the best long-term performing funds carry above-average costs – but are worth every penny.

The charges depend to some extent on the type of plan you buy and the structure of the fund, but they also vary from company to company. Life office charges are notoriously complex, which is why the Government is seeking to regulate certain pension and savings products to establish a benchmark for fair costs and terms. The Government is also keen to encourage more unit trust and investment trust groups to offer pension fund products in the hope that their simpler charging structures will make the product more flexible. However, the annual charges for unit trusts tend to be as high if not higher than the life offices, so simplicity does not automatically go hand-in-hand with low cost.

THE UNDERLYING ASSETS

There are several structures for individual pension funds – for example, unit-linked, unit trust, investment trust, conventional with-profits, 'unitised' with-profits and 'guaranteed' funds. Before you get bogged down with these confusing definitions, remember that all these funds invest in broadly the same range of asset classes – namely UK and overseas equities, gilts, bonds, cash (deposits) and in some cases property.

Your first consideration, therefore, is which asset classes are appropriate for you. These were discussed in Chapter 2. You should also consider carefully your attitude to risk and how this may change over the years. Certain structures – such as with-profits, lifestyle and guaranteed funds – offer an element of capital protection, but they achieve this in different ways, to different degrees of success and at a different cost to you, the investor.

Conventional wisdom suggests that younger people should invest virtually 100 per cent in equities because this offers the best long-term growth prospects. As you get older and closer to retirement, you need to switch gradually into safer assets, such as bonds and gilts, and by the time you are within a few years of retirement experts recommend that most people should be entirely in gilts and cash. Having said that, if you intend to transfer to an 'income drawdown' plan at retirement, which allows you to keep your fund fully invested, you will probably need to maintain a high exposure to equities. This high-risk retirement investment option is discussed on page 70.

UNIT-LINKED FUNDS

Unit-linked plans are sold by life offices. Under this arrangement your contributions buy units in a fund and the value of these units fluctuates in line with the market value of the underlying assets.

Funds range from low-risk deposit, index-linked and gilt, to medium-risk UK and international equity funds, all the way up to high-risk emerging markets funds. Some companies make much of their huge range of funds, but in practice most people go for the 'managed' fund which invests in a range of the provider's other main funds and in this way aims to offer a balanced spread of investments.

Charges vary depending on the type of fund. On average you can expect to pay an initial charge of about 5 per cent and an annual management charge of about 0.75 per cent to 1 per cent per annum. On top of this most regular premium plans have a monthly policy fee. Sales commission, where applicable, will affect the charges during the early years in particular and can effectively increase the initial charge to 30–40 per cent during the first two years on a long-term plan.

Remember, if you do pay commission, ask for your contributions to be classed as a series of single premiums or as 'recurring single premiums'. This means that each premium relates only to that particular payment so there are no heavy up-front deductions to cover commission costs for the full investment period. (*See* below and Chapter 1 for more details on charges.)

UNIT TRUST FUNDS

Unit trust plans are similar in principle to unit-linked plans in that the value of your units will fluctuate in line with the performance of the underlying assets. The choice of unit trust personal pensions was limited to about half a dozen at the time of writing, but more plans are expected to be launched over the next few years.

Unit trust companies do not usually pay a high up-front sales commission but instead pay a level amount per contribution. As a very rough guide, you can expect to pay a 5 per cent initial charge and anything up to 1.5 per cent for annual management. However, you can keep the bill down if you choose one of the index tracking funds that offer access to a wide spread of equities at low cost.

INVESTMENT TRUST PLANS

Over the past few years several investment trust personal pensions have been launched. An investment trust is not a trust as such, but is a UK company, listed on the stock exchange, which invests in the shares of other companies in the UK and overseas. It has a fixed number of shares and most prices are published daily in the *Financial Times*.

The investment trust's share price is affected by the value of the company's underlying assets – as is the case with unit-linked and unit trust funds. However, it is also affected by the supply and demand for shares. This means that the share price does not necessarily reflect the actual value of the underlying assets. If the share price is lower than the value of the underlying assets the difference is known as the discount. If it is higher, the difference is known as the premium. Broadly speaking, buying at a discount is a good thing. Investment trusts can also borrow money to invest – an activity known as gearing.

Charges tend to be lower than for unit trusts – particularly on some of the larger, older investment trusts.

Investment trusts are more interesting for the active investor but also potentially more volatile.

To summarise, investment trusts offer a similar range of investments to unit trusts and unit-linked funds but due to the impact of the premium/discount and the gearing, there are more variables. This means that investment trusts are more interesting for the active investor but also potentially more volatile.

WITH-PROFITS FUNDS

Until recently, traditional with-profits formed the backbone of the individual pensions market. These funds provided a reasonable degree of security, together with good potential for long-term capital growth. However, with-profits funds are ludicrously complicated, as those who manage to struggle through the rest of this section will discover.

The with-profits fund, like the managed unit-linked fund, invests mainly in UK and international equities, gilts and fixed-interest securities and property. Under the original with-profits contract (referred to by life offices as the 'traditional' or 'conventional' contract) the investor is guaranteed a substantial sum at the end of the agreed investment period (or 'maturity') to which annual bonuses are added. The important point here is that, rather like interest on a building society account, these bonuses, once allocated, cannot be taken away.

The annual bonuses are 'smoothed' in order to provide a relatively consistent return. To do this, the life office holds back some of the profits in good years to boost returns in lean years. In this way the plans aim to avoid the volatility associated with unit-linked and unit trust plans. On top of this there is a final or 'terminal' bonus which is discretionary and tends to reflect actual performance over the past 12 months.

This method of distributing profits to policyholders became more complex with the introduction of a two-tier annual bonus system. Originally bonuses were paid as a percentage of the sum assured plus any bonuses built up from previous years. Now, however, most providers allocate a lower bonus to the sum assured and a higher rate to the accrued bonuses.

A second trend in recent years has been for providers to place greater emphasis on the discretionary final bonus. Under some with-profits contracts, for example, the terminal bonus accounts for over 60 per cent of the total payout at maturity, while at the other end of the spectrum a terminal bonus may account for under 30 per cent of final fund.

Where the terminal bonus represents a significant proportion of the final fund, the risk level is higher since the payment is discretionary – not guaranteed – and reflects the recent performance of the fund. The other problem with this structure is that it is virtually impossible to predict the final fund size in the run-up to retirement, which makes it well nigh impossible to plan with any precision.

There are no explicit charges on a with-profits plan apart from a monthly policy fee. This does not mean that you don't pay charges; it simply means that you can't work out how they are calculated. Generally the charges are deducted from the fund itself before the bonuses are declared – again, rather like a building society account where charges are deducted before the interest rate is declared.

UNITISED WITH-PROFITS FUNDS

This is where the plot thickens to the point of total obscurity. Unitised with-profits plans are supposed to occupy the middle ground between the conventional with-profits structure and unit-linked funds. One advantage of this is that investors with unit-linked plans can more easily switch into the lower risk unitised with-profits fund – a common strategy in the run-up to retirement when you want to consolidate gains and reduce risk.

Unfortunately, when the life offices took this opportunity to revise their with-profit plans they paid little attention to the need for user-friendly design. Unitised plans are, if anything, even more complicated than their predecessors. Under unitised contracts there is no guaranteed sum assured and so the provider does not have to set aside such large reserves to meet its obligations. Furthermore, the bonuses are declared in a very different format from the traditional contract. Most providers increase the value of the unit price, but a minority maintain a fixed unit price and add bonuses through the allocation of extra units. Within these two systems there are a host of variations on the way profit is distributed. Quite a few providers do not offer a guaranteed minimum bonus at all.

As with the traditional contract, unitised funds also apply a final bonus, but the product has only been available for a few years and a clear pattern has not yet emerged.

Unitisation also heralded the arrival of the controversial 'market value adjuster' (MVA). This mechanism is used as a safety net for life offices in the event of a mass exodus of clients following a drop in the markets. Effectively the MVA allows a company to reduce the value of units if you pull out early. The MVA is not applied at retirement or on death.

Charges are similar to unit-linked plans.

THE NEW WITH-PROFITS FUNDS

A different type of with-profits fund was launched by Provident Mutual some ten years ago. Even though the product officially is classed as unit-linked, nevertheless it incorporates the concept of pooling investments and risk.

The fund, which was taken over by General Accident and now forms part of the CGU Life range, is valued at £1 billion and has over 100 000 investors. A similar product from Skandia was launched in May 1998. Both were designed by the same actuary. One clear distinction between the two products, however, is that the CGU fund is run in-house while the Skandia fund is split between four external institutional fund managers – Gartmore, Schroders, Newton and Perpetual. Skandia retains the flexibility to change the underlying asset allocation and the fund managers whenever this becomes necessary, without disturbing the guarantees.

The long-term nature of these funds enables managers to invest a high proportion in real assets – typically about 80 per cent in UK equities, overseas equities and property – with the rest in gilts, bonds and cash.

In both cases contributions buy units worth £1. There is no final bonus because all the growth of the fund is distributed each month as guaranteed bonuses in the form of further £1 units. This way, investors know exactly what their fund is worth at any given time. The charges are explicit (both have a 5 per cent bid offer spread, Skandia's annual charge is 1.2 per cent, CGU's 0.875 per cent) and the bonus calculations, if rather complex, are at least set out clearly in writing and appear genuinely to distribute all the profits.

The guarantee is that the full £1 value of units will be paid on death or the agreed retirement date. (An MVA can be applied if you pull out early.) The liabilities of these funds can be assessed accurately using actuarial methods and are met by keeping an appropriate proportion of the fund in liquid assets. Due to the clear bonus structure, payouts at maturity are a known quantity, while mortality tables are used to predict the level of death benefits that may be required at any given time.

Ultimately, however, the solvency of the fund could be undermined by a serious market crash followed by a prolonged bear market. In this case the life offices themselves act as guarantor by effectively reinsuring the risk. CGU uses a separate life fund to provide this guarantee while in Skandia's case it is provided by a with-profits fund owned by Skandia Liv, part of the Skandia Insurance Company group.

GUARANTEED EQUITY FUNDS

If you want the growth associated with equities but prefer to reduce your risks, you might consider one of the relatively new 'guaranteed' or 'protected' funds which limit your exposure to falls in the stock market but also limit the potential gains.

Guaranteed equity funds are strange beasts – they rarely invest in equities but instead hold mainly cash and gilts. The fund manager buys derivatives to guarantee a certain rise in the index and to limit the percentage of any fall in prices. Of course, the guarantee does not come free. In effect what you lose is the equivalent of the stock market dividend yield. When you consider the fact that over a ten-year period the yield on the FTSE 100 Index can account for roughly half of the total return, its absence seems a high a price to pay.

However, experts argue that you could be compensated for the loss of yield by the fact that the fund limits your exposure to any falls in the index, so you gain from potentially greater capital growth than unprotected investors. This is particularly relevant in volatile market conditions.

Charges are higher than for most of the other funds mentioned here – largely because of the cost of the derivatives that provide the guarantee.

Anything to do with derivatives is bound to be complicated and the jury is still out on whether these funds really do what they are supposed to do. If in doubt, remember the old saying: 'If you don't understand it, don't invest in it.' Having said that, there may be a strong argument in favour of using these funds for income drawdown plans, where you keep your pension fund fully invested in retirement (*see* page 70).

'If you don't understand it, don't invest in it.'

LIFESTYLE FUNDS

Lifestyle programmes aim to help you by taking the sting out of choosing the asset mix. Typically they achieve this by directing all your contributions into an equities fund until you are about ten years away from retirement. From this point your contributions and your fund are gradually switched from equities to gilts and cash.

Most experts agree that the lifestyle structure is the best default programme for investors who do not want to make their own asset allocation decisions or who might otherwise put too much into cash and bonds at an early age. There are drawbacks, however. Some advisers argue that to start to pull out of equities ten years before retirement takes you out of real assets (that is, assets which grow in value with the economy) too soon and at a time when regular premium plans in particular tend to benefit from the greatest growth. A five-year phased switch out of equities might be preferable.

Standard lifestyle programmes also do not cope well with the fact that most people do not know when they will retire. Few employees these days make it to the company retirement age. Most go early – either voluntarily or through a redundancy/early retirement programme. Self-employed businesses can also crash unpredictably, and health can decline, forcing early retirement. A decision to postpone retirement can be equally problematic for the lifestyle structure.

SELF-INVESTED PERSONAL PENSIONS

Self-invested personal pensions (SIPPs) are a variation on the basic personal pension contract and allow you to exercise much greater control over your investments. The appeal of the SIPP lies in the product's ability to separate the two key features of modern pension plans, namely the administration and the investment. The administration usually is carried out by a specialist life office and you either tackle the investment yourself or appoint an investment manager (a stockbroker, for example) to construct and run the portfolio for you. If you are unhappy with the performance, you can change the manager without having to upset the underlying administration arrangements.

SIPPs can also be used by partnerships. Schedule D taxpayers are excluded from the company sponsored small self-administered schemes (SSASs – *see* Chapter 13) but they can use a SIPP with virtually the same effect. For further details on SIPPs, *see* Chapter 5.

Key points

- Collective funds, whatever their structure, all invest in the same types of assets. Get your asset allocation right first, before considering the investment vehicle.
- Make sure your pension funds fit it with your other investments.
- Younger people should invest more in equities, but as you move towards retirement switch gradually into bonds and cash (deposits).
- Unit trusts and unit-linked funds link the value of your units directly to the value of underlying assets.
- Investment trusts are potentially more volatile than unit trusts.
- With-profits funds may offer valuable guarantees but are very complicated.
- Guaranteed equity funds use derivatives to limit a fall in value if the stockmarket crashes. They are useful in certain circumstances but can be expensive over the long term.
- Lifestyle funds automatically switch you from equities into bonds and cash in the run-up to retirement.
- Self-invested personal pensions allow you to invest in virtually any assets. You can change your stockbroker or investment adviser without changing the administration.

5

Personal pensions with greater investment scope

- Flexibility
- SIPPs: the rules
- Fee-based advice

Summary

One of the drawbacks with a standard personal pension is that in most cases you are restricted to the funds of just one institution. Given that your pension plan could run for 35–40 years if you start young, this hardly seems prudent. All it takes is for your star fund management team to defect to a rival company and your returns could plummet. Of course, if you are unhappy with the performance there is nothing to stop you transferring your plan to another pension company. Nothing, that is, except the exit penalties your pension company is likely to impose, particularly in the early years. On top of which you incur all the start-up costs with the new manager.

The Government hopes to improve this situation by introducing what it believes is a new breed of funds based on unit and investment trusts, which do not incorporate all the up-front deductions of the traditional life office products. However, while the charges under unit and investment trusts are easier to understand and more flexible, they are not necessarily lower than life office funds. Moreover, it is already possible to achieve greater investment flexibility and avoid the up-front charges. This chapter looks at these existing opportunities which hopefully will become more widely available as the Government encourages or even forces providers to offer genuine flexibility.

FLEXIBILITY

The simplest way to keep the whip hand is to steer clear of any contract terms that tie you to your pension company. There are two ways to avoid high up-front costs and/or exit penalties:

- Pay your adviser's charges by fees and ask for all commission payments to be stripped out of the contract. However, remember that you pay VAT on fees and there is no tax relief on these costs (*see* page 9). For this reason many fee-based advisers deduct their fee from the commission paid. This is fine in principle, but do check how the commission affects your flexibility.
- If you prefer the pension company to pay your adviser a sales commission, ask for 'single premium' terms. This means that each contribution is treated as a one-off and there are no large deductions in the early years to cover the adviser's charges over the full investment period. This is effectively what happens with unit and investment trusts.

If you do either of these, in theory at least your plan should be very portable. When investment performance loses its shine you pick up your plan and take it elsewhere. However, there would by necessity be certain administration charges for starting up a new plan, so you need to take into consideration two further options when you choose your plan.

Access to external managers

A cost-effective method of achieving a reasonable degree of investment flexibility without having to transfer to a new company every time performance flags is to choose a pension plan that provides access to a range of external managers as well as the company's own funds. This approach was pioneered by Skandia Life, but today about a dozen life offices offer external fund links and in future it is likely to become a standard feature. In the market so far, apart from Skandia, are Merchant Investors Assurance, Professional Life, Scottish Amicable, Scottish Equitable, Scottish Life and Winterthur Life.

However, do bear in mind that using a standard personal pension to gain access to institutional managers almost certainly will incur additional annual charges and therefore is more expensive than investing in a company's internal funds. Clearly, if this buys you superior performance and the flexibility to switch managers, it is well worth the extra cost.

DIY plans

For the dedicated investor there is an option that offers even greater investment flexibility. If you are paying about £10 000 or more each year into your plan it is well worth considering a self-invested personal pension (SIPP) which allows you to separate completely the administration and investment management so you can appoint your own investment manager (for example, a stockbroker) or even run the fund yourself. The beauty of this arrangement is that you can change your investment manager without disturbing the underlying administration and so cut out a significant layer of expense.

SIPPs are also good news for professional practices and partnerships (Schedule D taxpayers) who cannot join an occupational schemes. It is also possible to set up a group SIPP which may enable you to negotiate lower charges and achieve a greater degree of investment control on a collective basis.

SIPPs: THE RULES

SIPPs are available to employees who are not in company schemes, to the self-employed and to partnerships.

Self-invested personal pensions were introduced in the 1989 Budget to enable personal pension holders to manage their own investments. Like personal pensions, SIPPs are available to employees who are not in company schemes, to the self-employed and to partnerships. For full details on contribution and benefit limits refer to Chapter 4, page 39. Briefly, the amount you can pay in depends on your age and annual earnings. Contribution limits start at 17.5 per cent of total earnings for those up to age 35, rising in stages to 40 per cent for those over age 60. SIPPs can also be used to take transfers from other schemes.

Like all personal pensions, there is a monetary cap on the total earnings to which the contribution relates. This is £90 600 for the 1999–2000 tax year. The final pension, which is purchased in the form of an annuity from a life office, can be taken at any time between age 50 and 75. You can even keep your pension plan fully invested up to age 75 and draw an income directly from the fund through an 'income drawdown' plan (*see* page 70).

With a SIPP you need to buy the basic plan – often from a specialist life office which runs the administration. On top of this you can appoint an investment manager to run the investment portfolio. In theory it is possible to handle the investment management yourself but you should only undertake this task if you are an experienced investor and have the time to monitor stockmarkets on a regular basis.

Investment choice

The choice of investments is very wide and includes the following:

- stocks and shares (for example, equities, gilts, debentures) quoted on the UK stock exchange and including securities on the Alternative Investment Market;
- stocks and shares traded on a recognised overseas exchange;
- unit trusts and investment trusts;
- insurance company-managed funds and unit-linked funds;
- deposit accounts;
- commercial property.

A SIPP fund cannot purchase a firm's existing business premises from the partnership but it can buy new offices into which the partnership can move, provided the property is leased back on a commercial basis. You can also use your SIPP fund to borrow on the strength of its assets to help with property purchase. However, the SIPP cannot lend part of the pension fund back to you, the investor.

FEE-BASED ADVICE

The merits of fee-based advice, particularly where higher contributions are involved, are discussed in Chapter 1. A professional adviser, remunerated by fees, should be able to arrange nil commission terms on SIPPs where life office funds are used. Also, the higher premiums associated with SIPPs, particularly where they are arranged on a group basis, should make the fee approach cheaper in the long run. This is because conventional pension contracts that combine investment and administration normally make an initial charge based on a percentage of your contributions.

Key points

- **Look for a pension plan that offers a choice of external investment managers.**
- **For the bigger investor a self-invested personal pension (SIPP) allows you to separate the administration and asset management. You can run the fund yourself or appoint an expert to do this for you.**
- **Partnerships can set up a SIPP on a group basis and even use the fund to purchase new business premises.**

6

Annuities

- Your choice at retirement
- Conventional annuities
- Investment-linked annuities
- Phased retirement and income drawdown
- Conclusion and warning
- Voluntary annuities

Summary

An annuity provides a guaranteed income for life in return for a lump-sum investment. If you have a 'money purchase' (also known as 'defined contribution') pension arrangement, where the level of your pension is not linked to your salary, then most of the fund you build up must be used at retirement to buy an annuity to provide your retirement income. The annuity 'rate' is the amount of annual income your lump sum secures.

There is little point in spending hours of research in order to select the best personal pension if you fail to shop around for your annuity when you retire. The wrong choice could undo all the good work of the past. The top rates offered by the most competitive insurance companies can be 20–30 per cent higher than the bottom rates.

YOUR CHOICE AT RETIREMENT

If you have a money purchase pension, until recently when you wanted to withdraw your pension income you had to convert the whole of the fund (less the tax-free cash) to an annuity. Most annuities offer a fixed or rising income, but a handful offer an investment link to a with-profits or unit-linked fund, so here the level of income will be determined by how well your fund performs. There are very few investment-linked annuities around but they might be worth considering in the right circumstances. These products are discussed on page 69.

More recently two additional options – phased retirement and income drawdown – have been introduced to enable you to keep the bulk of your pension fund invested while you draw an income. For maximum flexibility some professional advisers recommend a combination of phased retirement and income drawdown. These arrangements can be ideal for the right type of investor, but for most people they are too complicated, expensive and risky (*see* page 70).

CONVENTIONAL ANNUITIES

Any discussion about annuities is rather ghoulish, so at this point you need to leave aside your natural squeamishness about mortality. Insurance companies are not charities. Their aim is to offer a good return for your money, but they still hope to make a profit. Early deaths make them very happy indeed.

The annuity 'rate' – or the level of regular income you secure in return for your lump sum – will depend on several important factors, including your life expectancy and interest rates (more precisely, on the yield on long-dated gilts). Women tend to live longer than men, so for a given fund they usually receive a lower income. If you are in ill health you may be able to get a better rate if the insurance company thinks your life expectancy is less than the average for your age. These are known as 'impaired life' annuities. Some companies also offer enhanced rates if you smoke and/or are overweight because, quite simply, they think you will die earlier than healthy people of the same age and sex.

Shop around with the 'open market option'

The first step towards choosing the right annuity is to use the 'open market option'. This allows you to take the proceeds of your pension fund away from the plan provider and to buy your annuity elsewhere.

The top names in personal pensions are quite different from the top names in annuities, so it pays to shop around. However, do take into consideration any penalties that affect your pension fund if you move it away from your original company. Alternatively, some companies pay 'loyalty bonuses' if you stay put, so your fund is worth less if you take it away.

You should also check whether your pension plan offers a guaranteed annuity rate. These were offered in the days of high inflation when the guarantee was considered laughably low. However, in a period of prolonged low interest rates as at present, some of these guarantees are very valuable.

Annuity options

The DSS applies certain rules to the type of annuity you must buy with the fund you build up from your rebates of National Insurance contributions. For example, you must buy a spouse's pension worth 50 per cent of your own and your income must be inflation linked (limited to a maximum increase of 5 per cent per annum).

With the rest of the fund there are no specific rules. However, there are several useful features that are sold as optional extras in addition to the basic annuity. Some of these may be essential, depending on your circumstances (but remember that they do reduce the annuity rate, so consider your priorities carefully).

- *Guaranteed annuities* guarantee to make payments typically for five years (although up to ten years is possible). If you die during this period your beneficiaries will receive the outstanding amount.

- *Joint life basis* means that a full or reduced pension will be paid to your spouse if you die.
- *Escalating annuities* rise in line with retail price inflation or at a fixed rate each year – typically 3 per cent or 5 per cent. Given you are likely to be retired for 20 years or more, some form of inflation proofing is essential, but the cost is rather prohibitive. A 5 per cent annual increase, for example, would reduce the initial annuity rate by about one-third. (If this sounds pricey, bear in mind that the purchasing power of £100 will be worth just £64 after 15 years of inflation at 3 per cent and £48 if the inflation rate is 5 per cent.)

Drawbacks with annuities

Annuities do have significant drawbacks which the income drawdown and phased retirement plans (*see* page 70) attempt to overcome. With a conventional annuity, once you hand over your money you cannot change your mind about the choice of insurance company or the special features selected. In most cases your money is gone for good, even if you die shortly afterwards. As mentioned above, you can protect your fund – usually for five years – but this costs extra.

INVESTMENT-LINKED ANNUITIES

In theory, investment-linked annuities offer the best of both worlds – the benefits of annuitising (that is, taking advantage of the cross subsidy from pooling risk) and of keeping the fund fully invested . This could represent a better deal for many investors who might otherwise be tempted by drawdown.

There are serious risks involved because your annual income is based on the return you expect your fund to achieve.

However, there are still serious risks involved because your annual income is based on the return you expect your fund to achieve. If it falls short you will deplete your fund too quickly, unless you reduce your income. So far, these products have restricted policyholders to just one company's funds. Some advisers would regard this as very risky because it is impossible to predict a company's ability to maintain good performance over the long term.

Another problem with these products is the lack of competition. There are very few life offices that offer an investment-linked annuity under the open market option. These include Equitable Life, the Prudential and Scottish Widows. Other life offices, such as Standard Life and Norwich Union, may well enter the investment-linked annuity market in due course. In addition, several providers – including M&G, Allied Dunbar and the former Provident Mutual (now part of CGU Life) – offer some sort of investment-linked annuity to existing pension clients.

PHASED RETIREMENT AND INCOME DRAWDOWN

There are two ways to put off buying your annuity. With phased retirement and income drawdown you take control of both the timing and the amount (within limits) of your income payments and at the same time keep your fund fully invested in a virtually tax-free environment.

Under phased retirement you generate your required annual income by withdrawing only part of your pension fund, leaving the remaining fund invested. The chunk withdrawn is used to provide an element of tax-free cash and the rest is used to buy a small annuity. The pattern is repeated each year. Phased retirement is not suitable for investors who want to use their tax-free cash for a capital project, as this is earmarked to generate part of your annual income. However, if you do not need the lump sum, phased retirement may be suitable. It also offers full tax-free cash to your beneficiaries on death (avoiding Inheritance Tax) and it can be easier to change your investment manager than under some of the packaged income drawdown plans, where this is only possible through the self-invested version.

Under income drawdown plans you can still take your tax-free cash as a single lump sum. You then draw your taxable income direct from your fund. The income level is flexible, although it must fall between a minimum and maximum set by the Inland Revenue, based broadly on the annuity rate you would otherwise have secured with your fund at retirement.

In both cases, your investments continue to grow free of Capital Gains Tax and virtually free of Income Tax. If you die, your fund goes to your dependants, not the insurance company, so there are important tax and financial planning benefits as well. By age 75 at the latest you must convert your fund to an annuity.

Investment risk

Of course, there is a catch. Income drawdown in particular is marketed as the ultimate in flexible retirement planning, but as any seasoned financial adviser will tell you 'flexible' in investment terms is synonymous with 'complicated', 'risky' and 'expensive'. Taking an investment risk while you are young may be perfectly acceptable, but it poses serious problems in retirement – when you have no earnings to fall back on if your savings are decimated by poor investment returns, high charges and substantial running costs. So, before you take the plunge, make sure you understand the downside of income drawdown as well as the potential benefits.

The main risk with these plans is that whereas with conventional annuities your pension income is guaranteed, with income withdrawal it is not. Neither is the position of your spouse if you die. If you do not purchase a guaranteed annuity with a spouse's pension at this stage then you should check your dependants are adequately protected if you die.

You might think that you could make your position more secure by investing in something fairly safe – gilts and deposits for example. However, in most cases this would defeat the object of the exercise, which is to generate a return that will match or improve the income you would have received from an annuity. Annuity rates are based on long-dated gilt yields, so you need to more than match this yield in order to meet your target growth. On top of this, your annual return must cover the cost of running the administration and investment management, which will be at least 1.5 per cent a year.

There is also a rather important but obscure factor called 'mortality drag' to consider. Basically, annuities work like an insurance pool – those who live get a cross subsidy from those who die. Under income withdrawal your beneficiaries get your money back if you die, so you lose this cross subsidy which experts reckon boosts conventional annuity rates by about 1.5 to 2 per cent a year. In total therefore, you are looking for returns of 3.5 per cent in excess of gilt yields. Based on historical returns, the only sensible way to achieve this is to invest in equities. And therein lies the rub. If markets fall your fund will plummet and take your retirement income with it. Clearly, if the fund was your only source of pension you could end up in deep trouble. The only way out would be to invest in even higher risk funds and then the white knuckle ride really starts.

For these reasons, advisers recommend that you should not consider phased retirement or income drawdown unless you have substantial funds. As a very rough guide, unless you have other sources of retirement income, you should not consider these arrangements with a fund size of less than £250 000. Some advisers put the figure at £500 000. Professional tax and investment advice is essential.

■ Types of income drawdown plan

There are several ways of setting up an income drawdown plan. You can buy an insurance company package that combines administration and investment management. However, once you take your tax-free cash and start to withdraw an income you cannot transfer your fund to another provider. If your plan restricts you to the internal funds of just one insurer, you are stuck with that company – and its investment performance – until you buy your annuity. This is quite a risk, given the fact that you could be investing for 15 to 20 years. Packaged products are sold by about 20 life offices, although several also offer a choice of external fund management links.

A second option, widely favoured by advisers, is to separate the administration and investment management and run the fund yourself or appoint an investment manager to do the job for you (rather like a self-invested personal pension – *see* Chapter 5). Under this type of plan you can invest in a very wide range of funds and asset classes including collective funds (investment trusts, unit trusts and insurance company funds), direct equities, bonds and commercial property. The administration normally would be carried out by an insurance company, although some financial institutions run their own plans and may also offer a discretionary investment management service.

A third option is to go for guaranteed funds which use derivatives to limit the downside of stockmarket risk – but at a price (*see* page 55).

Plan your exit

Finally, remember that the hallmark of good investment planning is knowing in advance when to get out. Under income withdrawal, by age 75 at the latest you must buy your annuity. To identify the best time to make your purchase you need to keep an eye on equity prices, which affect your fund size, and on gilt prices, which determine the level of income your annuity will provide. Generally, when equity prices go up, gilt prices also rise. This means gilt yields fall taking annuity rates with them.

The hallmark of good investment planning is knowing in advance when to get out.

So, what you want is a rise in equity prices and a fall in gilt prices – but it rarely works out that way. Clearly, trying to spot the right conjunction of equity and gilt movements is rather like astrology and best left to the experts.

Summary of income drawdown plan rules

If you have a personal pension or similar plan, at retirement you can take part of the fund (typically one-quarter) as tax-free cash and use the rest to buy an annuity. If you choose to defer the annuity purchase using a new income drawdown plan, the following rules apply:

- You can buy the plan from age 50 but must convert the fund to an annuity by age 75.

- If the plan is segmented, you may be able to make further pension contributions even when you are drawing an income.
- During the deferment period investment income and capital gains continue to roll up virtually tax free.
- The income you draw must fall between a minimum and maximum set by the Inland Revenue and be based on the annuity rate you would have purchased had you converted your fund at retirement.
- Your plan must be reviewed every three years to ensure the income level you are drawing is still appropriate. If the fund has fallen too much you must convert to an annuity immediately.
- If you die before age 75 there are three options:
  - your spouse can use the fund to buy an annuity;
  - your spouse can continue to draw an income but must convert the fund to an annuity by the time you would have reached 75;
  - the fund can be taken as cash (less a 35-per-cent tax charge).

CONCLUSION AND WARNING

Conventional annuities offer a rock-solid guarantee and represent the best option for those who will depend solely or mainly on this income. Shopping around for the best annuity rate certainly is essential.

Think very carefully before you commit yourself to an income drawdown plan – or similar arrangement – which exposes your retirement fund to stockmarket risks.

VOLUNTARY ANNUITIES

Most people come across annuities when they retire and have to buy a compulsory annuity with the proceeds of their pension fund.

There is, however, a second type, known as a 'purchased life' or 'voluntary' annuity, which anyone can buy with their spare capital. Having said that, the rates of income offered tend to be attractive only to the over-70s and probably are best value if you are in your late 70s or older. Younger people seeking extra income from their savings probably would be better off investing in a corporate bond or UK equity higher yielding individual savings account (ISA).

Unlike the income from compulsory annuities, which is taxed in full, only part of the income from a voluntary annuity is taxed. This is because the Revenue regards part of the payments as a return of the original capital and part as interest. Only the interest element is taxed. If you are a non-taxpayer it is possible to receive the whole of the annuity income tax free. Higher rate taxpayers should declare the interest element of the payments on the annual tax return.

Key points

- Do shop around – the best annuity rates can be 20–30 per cent more than the worst.
- Check if your pension company applies any penalties if you buy elsewhere or adds any loyalty bonuses if you stay put. Take these into consideration when shopping around.
- Do seek expert advice. Your adviser should specialise in annuities and have the necessary software to check all the products available.
- Consider carefully which features you need – for example, a spouse's pension and inflation proofing.
- Think carefully before opting for an investment-linked annuity since your income is not guaranteed and will fluctuate in line with investment returns.
- Consider income drawdown or phased retirement only if you have a substantial fund and other sources of income. Moreover, you must also feel comfortable with the equity market risks involved.

Further information

Several publications carry limited details of the best annuity rates on offer. These include *Moneyfacts*, the 'Weekend Money' section of the *Financial Times*, *Money Management*, *Planned Savings*, *Pensions Management* and *Pensions World*. For *Moneyfacts*, telephone 01603 476100. The rest are available through large newsagents.

7

Introducing company schemes

- Industry-wide and 'stakeholder' schemes
- How occupational schemes work
- Final salary schemes
- Money purchase company schemes
- Divorce
- Taxation in retirement

Summary

The UK has the most developed private pensions system in the European Union. Over 11 million employees and their families rely on company pension schemes, which in turn are backed by assets worth an estimated £755 billion.

For the vast majority of employees, membership of the company pension scheme represents the most important benefit after the salary itself. For a start, company schemes are tax efficient. The employer's contributions are tax deductible, the employee's contributions are paid free of basic and higher rate tax, the pension fund builds up virtually tax free and a significant chunk of the final benefits can be taken as tax-free cash at retirement. The pension itself is taxed as income.

Today more employees understand the nature of their schemes and the value of these benefits than in the past. But there are still many who fail to look beyond the monthly deductions from their pay cheque and naïvely assume that their employer will see them right. This is tantamount to leaving your financial security in retirement to luck. Some schemes provide very good pensions, while others will barely provide a subsistence income. The trick is knowing how to spot the difference and what to do if your scheme falls into the skimpy category.

INDUSTRY-WIDE AND 'STAKEHOLDER' SCHEMES

Occupational pensions are not limited to single-employer schemes. An increasing number of employers belong to industry-wide arrangements where a scheme is set up to cater for all employees within a specific sector – for example, broadcasting, chemical engineering, civil engineering, hotels and leisure groups, and so on.

The Government plans to extend the availability of such schemes through 'stakeholder' pensions so that employees and the self-employed who do not have access to a company pension can still join a group scheme. This initiative, announced in a pensions Green Paper in December 1998, is very welcome. Group arrangements generally offer economies of scale that cannot be achieved by individual plans.

Stakeholders will be a special type of industry-wide scheme which will meet certain Government guidelines on charges, flexibility and terms. Many existing industry-wide schemes already broadly meet these requirements.

If your company does not offer its own pension scheme then it makes sense to consider an industry-wide or, in due course, a stakeholder scheme. This should offer better value than an individual personal plan, which can be expensive to set up and administer.

HOW OCCUPATIONAL SCHEMES WORK

Despite the complicated rules and regulations, the basic principles of company schemes are really quite straightforward. However, you may have to persevere if you want to get clear information out of your pensions manager or trustees. A spot of background knowledge will stand you in good stead. But first, *see* Table 7.1 for a few facts and figures.

Table 7.1 Facts about company pensions

Number of employees covered by occupational schemes:	11 million, plus their families
Total working population:	28 million, of which 23 million are employed
Total value of funds:	£755 billion
Typical employee contribution rate:	5 per cent (final salary); 3.5 per cent (money purchase)
Non-contributory schemes:	24 per cent
Company schemes run on a money purchase basis:	15–20 per cent
Schemes that can provide unmarried partners' pensions (at trustees' discretion):	66 per cent (private sector); 15 per cent (public sector)

Source: National Association of Pension Funds

Trust law

Occupational pension schemes are based largely on trust law but this framework was reinforced by statutory regulations introduced by the Pensions Act 1995. Although rather quirky at times, there are three good reasons for using trust law as the basis for pension schemes:

- *To separate the pension fund from the rest of the company's assets*. In theory this keeps the fund safe, for example from predators if the company is the subject of a hostile take-over or from creditors if the company goes bust.
- *To manage money on behalf of others*. In the case of a pension fund the money is managed on behalf of the scheme members and other beneficiaries who, for tax reasons, cannot get their hands on their pension until normal retirement date.
- *To obtain Inland Revenue approval to qualify for tax purposes*.

Trustees and beneficiaries

You can't have a trust without a trustee who, as legal owner of the fund, is obliged to look after the assets on behalf of the beneficiaries. In the case of pension funds the beneficiaries are:

- the scheme members;

- retired scheme members drawing pensions;
- ex-employees with deferred pensions (pension benefits they left behind when changing jobs);
- the dependants (spouses and children) of all three categories.

Historically, employers drew most of their trustees from the management team but clearly this could, and sometimes did, lead to abuse. If the company was cash poor but pension fund rich it could be tempting for the management trustees to use the fund to bolster up the company's flagging finances.

To improve the balance of power on trustee boards, from April 1997 scheme members have the right (but not the obligation) to appoint one-third of the trustee board from their ranks. In practice, of course, their presence alone will make little difference if they do not understand the job. It requires a trained eye to spot pensions skulduggery in the making, so if you are thinking of becoming a member trustee be sure to insist on some proper training for the job.

Pensions Act 1995

The Act, which came into force in April 1997, followed a widespread overhaul of pensions legislation in the wake of the Robert Maxwell scandal, when millions of pounds went missing from his company's pension fund. The legislation generally is aimed to improve the security of pension funds by introducing a new series of checks and balances, and by appointing a pensions regulator.

With a money purchase scheme the investment risk falls fairly and squarely on your shoulders.

The main types of pension scheme

There are two main types of occupational schemes – 'final salary' (also known as 'defined benefit') and 'money purchase' (also known as 'defined contribution'). With a final salary scheme the investment risk and guarantees are backed by the employer. With a money purchase scheme the investment risk falls fairly and squarely on your shoulders as the scheme member and there are no guarantees. Not surprisingly, money purchase schemes are proving very popular with employers.

FINAL SALARY SCHEMES

Final salary schemes, still the most prevalent among employers in the UK, base the pension calculation on the number of years of service and your salary at or near retirement. Rather oddly, for what is essentially a tax-efficient investment, this means there is no direct link between what you pay in and what you get out. This explains much of the confusion that arises with these schemes.

A typical scheme might guarantee to provide a pension that builds up at the rate of one-sixtieth of your final salary for each year of service, up to an Inland Revenue maximum of forty-sixtieths – that is, two-thirds final salary at retirement (restricted for some higher earners). Some schemes operate on an 'eightieths' basis where the employee builds up one-eightieth of final salary for every year of service and after 40 years has achieved a pension worth forty-eightieths or one half of final salary.

As if this were not complicated enough, public sector schemes usually operate on an eightieths basis but are regarded as equivalent in value to a 'sixtieths' scheme because the tax-free cash is paid in addition to the pension, not instead of part of the pension, as is the case with private sector schemes.

A minority of schemes – usually only those aimed at senior management – are more generous and build up at the rate of one-thirtieth of final salary for each year of service, allowing the employee to achieve a maximum two-thirds pension after just 20 years.

In 1988 – the year personal pensions were introduced – companies lost the right to make membership of their schemes a condition of employment, although in most cases it will be in your best interests to join. Some companies operate an automatic membership system, so if for some reason you do not want to join you have the right to opt out. The Government is likely to reintroduce compulsory membership for employees in its bid to increase private pension coverage.

Employee contributions

Employees can contribute up to 15 per cent of gross pay to an occupational scheme although the most common rate is about 5 per cent. 'Pay' in this context is defined as basic salary plus benefits such as overtime, bonuses and the taxable value of fringe benefits.

The proportion of your earnings on which you can base your contributions will vary from scheme to scheme. Some schemes provide a pension linked to basic pay while others take into account the other elements that make up gross pay, including, for example, regular overtime or sales-related commission. If overtime forms a significant proportion of your gross earnings, and this is not taken into account in your pensionable pay, you could consider top-up provision through additional voluntary contributions or some other tax-efficient investments (*see* Chapter 8).

The definition of 'pensionable pay' is particularly important, since the final pension will also be calculated on this basis. For example, many schemes base the pension on your average salary during the last three years before retirement. If this is the case you should think twice before accepting a less onerous but lower paid position in the run-up to retirement. Other employers link the pension to the employee's average salary during the period of scheme membership or, in some cases, to the period of maximum earnings. The latter system is ideal if you are in a job where earnings peak mid-career rather than towards the end of the working life.

Employer contributions

The employer's contributions are an extremely valuable perk. Where employers pay a fixed rate in a generous scheme this may be worth twice the value of the employees' contributions. In practice, however, employers tend to vary their contributions according to what the scheme actuary calculates must be invested, so the fund can pay the pensions and benefits guaranteed by the scheme. As a result, employers tend to pay more on behalf of older employees approaching retirement than for younger employees who have 30–40 years to go.

Restrictions for higher earners

Over the past five years the Revenue has restricted the pensions of certain high earners. In particular, some employees are subject to a cap of £90 600 for the 1999–2000 tax year, on which contributions and the final pension can be based. The cap applies to members of final salary schemes set up after the 1989 Budget and members who joined any final salary scheme after 1 June 1989. For these employees the maximum contributions for the 1999–2000 tax year are £13 590 (15 per cent of the cap), while the maximum pension will be £60 400 (two-thirds of the cap). Pension options for 'capped' employees are discussed in Chapter 9.

In practice very few people end up with the maximum permitted pension, so most will benefit from AVCs.

Topping up your company pension

By law every scheme, with a few minor exceptions, must provide an additional voluntary contribution (AVC) scheme which allows members to top up their company pension. In practice very few people end up with the maximum permitted pension, so most will benefit from AVCs.

Since 1987, employees also have been able to contribute to individual top-up plans known as free-standing AVCs (FSAVCs), which are sold by insurance companies and other financial institutions. As a general rule, the company AVC scheme will offer better value. You might also consider individual savings accounts (ISAS) for retirement income planning. These options are discussed in Chapter 8.

Transfers

The complex topic of pension transfers is dealt with in Chapter 10.

Company pension age

Due to the influence of European Union law, company schemes, like the State scheme, are moving towards an equal pension age for men and women. The most common practice is for schemes to raise the female pension age from 60 to the male pension age of 65. This would normally be phased in over a fairly long period to avoid disadvantaging those women in their 50s who expect to qualify for a full pension at age 60.

There are some variations on the theme. Some schemes have lowered the male pension age so that both sexes can retire at 60, but due to the cost this is rare. Others have equalised at 63, while a further group have introduced a 'flexible' period for retirement during which employees can take their pension. However, 'flexible' schemes still normally set an age at which full pension is payable: if you go early then your pension would be reduced.

As a general rule, if you take voluntary early retirement your pension will be reduced because your contribution period was shorter than expected and the employer expects to pay the pension over a longer period. Sometimes employers waive these reductions for early retirement on the grounds of ill health or if the company is looking for volunteers in a redundancy programme.

Value of State pension deducted

About 50 per cent of company schemes reduce the pension by 'integrating' with the basic State pension. The idea behind this is to provide a maximum two-thirds final salary pension including the State benefit. Of course, it also cuts company pension costs. The important point to remember is that where a scheme is integrated, no pension is paid for the first slice of salary up to the NI lower earnings limit (£3432 in 1999–2000), but no employee or employer pension contributions are levied on this amount either.

Equal pensions

In the past, men generally received a better pension and related benefits package than women, because it was assumed they were the main breadwinners. This meant that, for example, a scheme would pay a death-in-service lump sum and pension to a member's widow, but the widower of a female scheme member might get little or nothing if his spouse died.

Under European Union law it is now firmly established that women should have equal pay for equal work and that pension forms part of pay. It is illegal to exclude women from pension schemes in most circumstances and from October 1994 women who take maternity leave should be covered for this period by their pension scheme.

Contracting out

Most final salary schemes are contracted out of the State Earnings-Related Pension Scheme (SERPS). As a result the employer and, in most cases, employees pay a reduced rate of National Insurance contribution, with the balance invested in the company pension fund.

Until April 1997 these schemes had to guarantee to provide a pension at least as good as the SERPS benefit given up. This element of the company pension, which effectively replaced most of the SERPS pension, was known as the 'guaranteed minimum pension' (GMP). For service after April 1997, however, employers no longer have to provide a guaranteed pension in replacement for SERPS.

Where the scheme is not contracted out the employee would receive the SERPS pension and the company pension on top of this.

Tax-free cash

The maximum tax-free cash you can take from your company pension scheme is one and a half times your final salary after 40 years' service. This is limited in the case of some higher earners (*see* page 84). If you are in a private sector scheme and you take the tax-free cash your pension will be reduced.

Pension increases

Most company schemes increase pensions by 3–5 per cent each year. However, you need to check which increases are guaranteed and which are not. Voluntary payments by the fund are known as 'discretionary' increases. Public sector pensions automatically increase in line with inflation.

Family protection benefits

Most final salary schemes provide other important family protection benefits in addition to the pension itself. For example, death-in-service benefits can be paid of up to four times annual salary (the typical rate is two or three times salary), a widow's or widower's pension may be paid, plus dependent children's pensions and similar death-in-retirement benefits. Disability pensions and private medical insurance are also common features of the overall benefits package.

If the family protection insurances offered by your scheme are on the low side, it may be necessary to boost your life cover, either through some form of family income benefits plan, which pays an annual amount for a selected period of time, or a lump-sum life assurance policy. Both types of insurance are available from life offices in return for relatively modest monthly premiums. Shop around for the best rates, preferably through an independent adviser.

Benefits for unmarried partners

Scheme members with unmarried partners, whether of the opposite or the same sex, often are the subject of discrimination if the scheme rules only permit death benefits and survivor pensions to be paid to the lawful spouse.

Usually it is possible to nominate the person to whom your death-in-service benefits should go and these nomination forms remain sealed until your death, so that gay and lesbian scheme members do not have to disclose details of their private lives. Payment of the pension to anyone other than the lawful spouse is more difficult to arrange, although some schemes have introduced rules to allow partners' pensions to be paid to common law spouses. Usually though, payment may only be made provided the relationship was long term and a significant degree of financial interdependency can be proved.

If you want to find out your position under your own scheme rules, look in the scheme booklet and if this is not clear, contact the trustees. The State scheme only pays pensions to spouses.

Pension fund investment

Under a final salary scheme the employee and employer contributions go into a central trust fund which is legally separate

How well the fund performs often dictates the future level of contributions and benefits.

from the assets owned and controlled by the company. The legal owners of the fund are the trustees who, as explained above, look after the assets on behalf of the beneficiaries. The trustees are expected to delegate the day-to-day investment management to professionals. How well the fund performs often dictates the future level of contributions and benefits, particularly with regard to discretionary pension increases (increases that are not guaranteed by the scheme but which the trustees feel the fund is capable of paying).

Most large pension schemes are 'self-administered', which means that the fund management is separate from the administration. However, both functions can be carried out by specialists who work directly for the pension fund. Smaller schemes, and these include many money purchase schemes (*see* page 89), tend to be run by life offices which offer a combined investment and administration service, although where the fund management is handled by a unit or investment trust group, a third party usually is appointed for the administration.

The good company pension scheme

Most people assume that if they join their company pension scheme it will provide a decent level of retirement income and other related benefits, but in practice final salary terms and benefits vary considerably. The same is true of money purchase schemes, discussed on page 89. If you want to check how well your company pension scheme rates, consult your scheme booklet and compare the benefits with our ideal scheme listed below.

A good final salary scheme might offer:

- A pension of two-thirds final salary after a maximum of 40 years, not taking account of the State pension.
- A pension based on total earnings not just basic pay.
- Suitable arrangements for high earners whose pensionable salary is capped (for members who join a scheme set up after the 1989 Budget or who joined any scheme from 1 June 1989, the

maximum salary on which contributions and the benefits are based is £90 600 in 1999–2000).

- Annual pension increases in line with retail prices.
- A death-in-retirement pension for partner (not just the narrower definition of 'spouse') of two-thirds your own, plus a pension for children under 18.
- A death-in-service pension for your partner and children under 18, plus a lump sum of three times annual salary (the Revenue maximum is four times salary).
- An ill-health pension equivalent to the amount you would have received if you had continued to retirement age at the same rate of pay.
- If you change jobs, an increase in the whole of the 'preserved' pension you leave with your former employer, in line with retail prices up to retirement.

Source: Based on Union Pension Services 'Pension Scheme Profiles'

Well-run pension schemes have always tried to ensure that members understand the way their pension works and are kept informed of important developments. However, regulations under the Social Security Act 1985 introduced a legal requirement for trustees to provide members with certain information (known as disclosure regulations). This requirement was updated by the Pensions Act 1995.

The trustees should provide the basic scheme information automatically to all prospective members, preferably before they join, but if not then within two months of joining. This should cover all the details listed in the 'good company pension scheme' guide above. It should also explain other points, such as the internal dispute resolution procedure.

MONEY PURCHASE COMPANY SCHEMES

There is a growing trend among employers in the UK to switch from final salary pension schemes to money purchase, or to introduce a money purchase option. Money purchase schemes allow employers to control their costs and also to transfer the investment risk to you, the scheme member. Now, this is not necessarily a bad thing, but you do need to check the calibre of the administration and investment management companies running the pension scheme before joining. There are some excellent money purchase schemes around, run by top firms of employee benefit consultants and investment managers. But some insurance companies sell poor-quality schemes which combine dismal performance with high charges and inflexible contract conditions. Clearly, you need to know how to spot the difference.

One of the arguments employers use to justify the switch to money purchase is that employees do not understand final salary schemes and therefore do not appreciate them. They are absolutely right – if you made your way through the first part of this chapter you can see why. However, one very important feature of final salary schemes is that your employer is responsible for backing the pension guarantee and is obliged to contribute a variable amount to the pension fund to keep it solvent and able to meet its liabilities.

Money purchase schemes can be attractive, especially for younger employees, because you have an identifiable pot of money which you should be able to take from job to job. Contributions are invested to build up a fund which, at retirement, is used to buy an annuity from an insurance company. An annuity pays an income for life in return for a lump sum. The most important point to bear in mind with money purchase is that, like personal pensions (*see* Chapter 4), the level of income your fund buys is not guaranteed but will depend on four factors:

- how much you and your employer contribute;
- the investment performance of the fund;
- the level of charges deducted from your fund by the pension company;
- annuity 'rates' – the level of income your fund will buy at the time you retire (annuity rates are based on the yields of long-dated gilts – *see* Chapter 6).

Companies which introduce money purchase schemes do so in many different ways. Some employers close the old scheme and direct all future contributions to the new scheme. However, it is more common to introduce the money purchase scheme for new employees and offer existing scheme members the choice. In some cases the money purchase scheme will be open to younger employees who can join the final salary scheme when they are older.

Bear in mind that pension transfers are notoriously complicated. If you are offered the chance to transfer your existing benefits from the old scheme to the new, do ask an independent pensions adviser or your trade union to check if it is a fair deal (and *see* Chapter 10).

The good money purchase scheme

Use the following checklist to find out if your employer's money purchase scheme is well designed. It should:

- Aim (but it cannot guarantee) to match the pension and risk benefits equivalent to a good final salary scheme (*see* above).
- Invest minimum employer and employee total contributions of between 10–15 per cent of annual salary, depending on age. (You will need to pay more if you have not been contributing to a pension scheme all your working life.)
- Delegate the investment management to an institutional fund manager that has a proven track record in the pensions market.
- Incur competitive administration and investment management charges.
- Impose no financial penalties if you leave the scheme when you change jobs, you reduce contributions, or you want to retire early.

If you don't want to make the investment decisions your scheme should also offer a 'lifestyle' option (*see* page 56). This directs your contributions into equities in the early years to provide maximum potential for capital growth, but protects your fund as you approach retirement by automatically phasing a gradual switch from equities into cash and bonds.

Life cover under money purchase

Life cover under a money purchase scheme should include a benefit linked to salary – for example, three times annual salary. However, you may just be offered a return of your fund. If you have only been in the scheme a short while this will not provide much of a pension for your spouse, so it may be wise to increase your life assurance during the early years while the fund builds up.

Topping up

In most cases it is worthwhile joining your employer's scheme even if it offers skimpy benefits. This is because you will benefit from the company's contributions and, hopefully, the lower costs achieved through economies of scale. Remember, employers can contribute to your personal pension plan but they are under no obligation to do so. If you think you will not build up a decent pension you could top it up by increasing contributions to the main scheme or by paying additional voluntary contributions (AVCs – *see* Chapter 8).

In most cases it is worthwhile joining your employer's scheme even if it offers skimpy benefits.

Types of money purchase scheme

To some extent the precise nature of the money purchase scheme is immaterial, but for those who want to understand the small print, the following descriptions may help. Most money purchase schemes fall into one of three categories:

Group personal pensions (GPPs) are probably the simplest and most popular type of money purchase scheme for employers. They also attract the largest rebates of national insurance contributions for those who want to contract out of SERPS. GPPs are not classed as occupational schemes by the Revenue and in practice they operate in the same way as individual plans, although a well-designed scheme should offer some economies of scale.

Under a GPP, your individual personal pension plan can be used to contract out of SERPS and to invest additional regular or single premiums to boost the pension provided by the NI rebate. Personal pension contribution limits start at 17.5 per cent of 'net relevant earnings' (equivalent in this context to pensionable pay) for employees up to age 35, and rising to 40 per cent for employees age 61 and over (*see* page 39). Employer contributions must be included in these limits, but there is no obligation for employers to pay anything. The retirement income provided by the personal pension is not linked to final salary. Death-in-service benefits are not compulsory, although the personal pension itself may provide a return of contributions plus interest. Extra life assurance can be taken out to increase this benefit.

Contracted-out money purchase schemes (COMPs) are Inland Revenue-approved occupational pensions and as such will follow the same contribution and benefit limits as final salary schemes. These limits are not guarantees – what you actually get will depend on the size of your fund at retirement and annuity rates. A COMP scheme must have a trust deed and rules and there must be a board of trustees who, as with final salary schemes, must provide annual accounts and are there to protect the interests of scheme members. COMPs are contracted out of the State Earnings-Related Pension Scheme (SERPS) and in return receive a rebate of employee and employer National Insurance (NI) contributions.

Contracted-in money purchase schemes (CIMPs) are similar to COMPs but employees remain in SERPS and the scheme provides benefits on top of this State pension. Younger employees can join a CIMP and contract out of SERPS on an individual basis using an 'appropriate' personal pension plan in order to receive the NI contribution rebate (*see* Chapter 3).

Contribution level

Money purchase schemes can match or even exceed final salary pensions provided large enough contributions are paid. Unfortunately, however, in the early days these arrangements earned a reputation for providing employers with a cheap alternative to final salary schemes and in some cases the combined employer/employee contribution is too low to provide an adequate pension. (For an idea of what you should be paying, *see* Table 3.2 on page 40.)

Contribution matching

'Contribution matching' in money purchase schemes is a valuable feature. The scheme basis might, for example, require a contribution of 5 per cent from both employer and employee. On top of this some employers guarantee to match any further contribution the employee makes up to an agreed limit.

The scheme provider

An increasing number of institutional managers are coming in to the money purchase market. These managers tend to delegate administration to a third party specialist. However, most money purchase pensions are still run by insurance companies which normally provide both administration and investment services combined.

Your employer should have taken expert independent advice and conducted a thorough analysis of different providers' financial strength, the management and commission charges, administration facilities, flexibility of contract terms and investment track record. If your employer accepted advice from a direct salesman or tied agent they would have received details about only one provider.

The charges

The scheme provider's charges will have a direct impact on the investment return and flexibility of your pension scheme. Where a standard life office package is used there may be large deductions in order to pay the high commission costs to the salesman or adviser, on top of which there will be administration and investment charges. Many advisers are prepared to rebate part or all of the commission in return for a fee, and some will only work on a fee basis so there is no deduction for commission. A good adviser will establish the most cost-effective contribution method.

Flexibility and portability

Flexibility is supposed to be one of the main attractions of money purchase pensions since the employee has an easily identifiable and apparently portable pot of money. The important point to

Check what happens to your fund if you leave the scheme when you change jobs.

check here is what happens to your fund if you leave the scheme when you change jobs.

Long-term, regular premium life office contracts are notorious for their early termination penalties. Ideally your contract should have been established on a nil-commission basis or, alternatively, contributions should be paid on a 'recurring single premium' basis – a series of one-off investments – since the up-front charges are modest and there are no early termination charges.

DIVORCE

For most married couples the main breadwinner's company pension scheme benefits form the most valuable possession after the family home. Where the house is still mortgaged its net value often falls below that of the pension. Over one-third of marriages in the UK end in divorce but until 1996 there was no legal obligation to split the main breadwinner's (usually the husband's) pension fairly. Instead, in England and Wales, pension rights were dealt with at the discretion of the courts. In contrast, the law in Scotland is clear. Under the Family Law (Scotland) Act 1985 'matrimonial property' specifically includes the proportion of pension and insurance rights accumulated during marriage, and in most cases these must be divided equally between the partners.

The law in England and Wales is set to change. Since July 1996 the courts have been able to earmark the spouse's share of the pension and this will be paid out at retirement. Some time after 2000 (the precise date is not yet known), the court should be able to demand an immediate split of the funds so the lower earning spouse can invest his or her share of the pension into a personal pension fund.

This whole areas is very complex and you should seek professional advice on the calculation of your pension rights, particularly if you or your spouse have built up a substantial pension.

TAXATION IN RETIREMENT

The pension, whether drawn from a company scheme or from a life office in the form of an annuity, is subject to income tax. As you come up to retirement it is important that you tell your tax office so that it can adjust your tax code. If you are over 65 you can claim a higher allowance, and this increases again when you reach 75. Clearly, if you continue working part time in retirement, your total income will be taxed, including your pensions. For full details on your tax position, contact your local tax office, providing details of your date of birth and your tax reference.

Key points

- **It is almost always in your best interests to join your employer's pension scheme.**
- **If your employer does not run a scheme, check if there is an industry-wide scheme which you can join. Your employer or trade union should be able to point you in the right direction.**
- **Use the good pension scheme guides in this chapter to see where your employer's scheme falls short.**
- **If necessary top up your pension with additional voluntary contributions, free-standing AVCs or individual savings accounts.**
- **Make sure your family protection benefits are adequate; if not, top up with private insurance arrangements.**

Further information

The Inland Revenue publishes useful leaflets, including *Income Tax and Pensioners, Income Tax – A Guide to Tax Allowances and Reliefs* and several others. All tax offices have a stock of these leaflets and they will be happy to send these to you. Alternatively you could try your local library or Citizens Advice Bureau.

The National Association of Pension Funds publishes a series of leaflets on company schemes and related issues. Many of these will be available free of charge from your pensions manager, but if not write to the Association for a guide to its publications: NAPF, 12–18 Grosvenor Gardens, London SW1W 0DH. Tel: 0171 730 0585. Fax: 0171 730 2595.

The Trades Union Congress also publishes useful fact sheets on company pensions. Write to the TUC, Congress House, Great Russell Street, London WC1B 3LS. Tel: 0171 636 4030. Fax: 0171 636 0632.

8

Topping up your company pension

- Why do you need to top up?
- Tax-efficient top-ups
- Company AVCs
- Free-standing AVCs
- Contribution and benefit limits
- Investment options
- Flexibility
- Individual savings accounts

Summary

Only one in ten employees in company pension schemes retires on the full level of pension permitted by the Inland Revenue, yet very few take advantage of a readily available, tax-efficient method of topping up their retirement income.

Pension top-up plans are known as 'additional voluntary contributions' (AVCs), where they are run by the company pension scheme, and the even more unwieldy title 'free-standing additional voluntary contributions' (FSAVCs), where they are set up on an individual basis by the employee. Generally, the in-house AVC scheme will be your best option because group schemes tend to be more economical and the employer usually bears some or all of the running costs. FSAVCs, by contrast, can be expensive.

As always, however, it is important to look at the overall retirement income and not just investments labelled 'pensions'. The individual savings account (ISA) is particularly suitable for long-term savings and is likely to be a cheaper, more flexible alternative to FSAVCs. The merits of ISAs v. FSAVCs are discussed on page 111. You can and should consider paying into both an AVC/FSAVC and an ISA in order to get the most out of the available tax breaks and to improve the flexibility of your retirement savings.

WHY DO YOU NEED TO TOP UP?

As we saw in the last chapter, to get a full company pension – limited to two-thirds of your final salary – usually it is necessary to work for 40 years for the same employer. This is because most company pensions build up at the rate of one-sixtieth of final salary for each year of service and the maximum is forty-sixtieths or two-thirds (restricted in the case of some higher earners). Bearing this in mind, the reasons for gaps in pension provision are not hard to find in today's world of flexible careers, redundancies, job changes and early retirements.

Here are some of the reasons why you may not end up with a full pension and will need to take action:

- periods of unemployment or additional years spent as a student;
- a career break to raise a family or look after a dependent relative;
- periods of self-employment;
- one or more job changes that involved transfers of pensions;
- membership of a scheme where the pension builds up at a low rate;
- a large proportion of earnings, for example, bonuses or overtime, is not taken into account for pension purposes;
- the company scheme is integrated with the State scheme, so you do not build up a pension to cover the first £3500-plus of salary;
- late entry age to the company scheme;
- early retirement (voluntary or enforced).

It's worth looking in more detail at each case to see why a pension shortfall arises.

Periods out of employment

It doesn't really matter if it's unemployment, further education or a career break to have a family – whatever the reason for periods out of employment the result is likely to be a significant underfunding of your pension. Fortunately it is likely that in most of these situations you would qualify for help towards the State pension, but (as explained in Chapter 15) this is a low level of benefit and in no way compensates for a good occupational scheme.

Self-employment

There are some excellent pension options for the self-employed, including individual personal pensions, pensions for partnerships and small company schemes (see Chapters 4, 5, and 13) but the fact remains that many self-employed people overlook their pension arrangements for long periods due to the financial strain of building up a business. Those who are 'between jobs' and fill in the time with some self-employed work also tend to ignore pensions, even when a temporary break ends up lasting for several years.

Whatever you do with your pension rights, the very act of changing jobs is likely to create a shortfall.

Job changes

Pension transfers, examined in detail in Chapter 10, affect most of us at some time in our careers. Occupational pension schemes evolved in the days when employers took a paternalistic attitude towards employees (if you were lucky) and rewarded loyalty for long service with a pension for old age. You don't have to go back very far to the days when the traditional pattern for employment was to start as an apprentice and to spend your entire working life with the same employer. Clearly this pattern is no longer the norm. The average number of job changes in a 40-year career is between five and seven, which means that some people may change only once or twice, while others may have ten or more jobs during their working lives.

If you leave an employer you can take your pension rights with you to the next scheme, but for various reasons – some perfectly reasonable and others less so – your 'transfer value' is likely to be worth less than your benefits were really worth in the old scheme while you were still a member and working for that employer. You can leave your pension benefits where they are as a 'deferred pension' (a pension where the payment is deferred or put off until your retirement) but it will not increase each year by the full rate of earnings inflation. (Again, for full details on this important topic, see Chapter 10). Whatever you do with your pension rights, the very act of changing jobs is likely to create a shortfall.

Low company scheme benefits

While the most common rate for the pension to build up in an occupational scheme is one-sixtieth of final salary for each year of service (and some executive schemes build up more quickly), there are schemes that build up at the rate of one-eightieth of final salary for each year of service. Clearly in this situation, where the company pension age is 65, it is impossible to achieve a full two-thirds final salary pension – unless you are prepared to work for 53 years with the same company!

Company earnings not taken into account

To a large extent your employer has a free hand in deciding which elements of your earnings form the basis for pension contributions and benefits. Often this is restricted to the basic salary and does not take into account additional regular income such as bonuses, overtime and other non-basic pay. For shift workers or employees who receive a significant proportion of their earnings as overtime, or as sales or performance bonuses, this can lead to a pension based on a much lower income than is actually received.

Value of State scheme deducted

About two and a half million people are in company schemes which are 'integrated' with the State scheme. This reduces the value of the final pension by a minimum of about £3500 and often much more. This is because the maximum pension calculation of two-thirds final salary used by the scheme assumes that the State pension will be paid in full and excludes this tier of earnings from pensionable pay. What the employer does is to deduct from the employee's salary the value of the State pension or the 'lower earnings limit' (LEL) for National Insurance contributions – £3432 in 1999–2000. Some employers deduct one and a half or twice this integration factor, which can mean that you will receive no pension for the first £5148–£6864 of your salary. Higher earners may hardly notice the difference but for lower earners the impact is very significant. Moreover, as is explained in Chapter 15, not everyone qualifies for the full basic State pension.

Late entry age to scheme

Some employers are reluctant to let young employees join the pension scheme if they operate in an industry where there is a high turnover of young staff. Computer workers, the leisure industry, retail sales staff and journalists are classic examples. To cut costs and administration such companies commonly set a high entry age to the pension scheme, often at or around 30 (the age at which employees miraculously are expected to become more settled in their careers). The problem here is that unless you had the foresight to take out a personal pension to cover the intervening years, you will end up with a maximum of 35 years in the scheme – less if you change jobs – and hence a lower pension than you might otherwise have expected.

In a welcome move, some employers have introduced a money purchase scheme for younger workers which provides a good start to their pension but in a simpler and more portable format than the main final salary scheme.

Early retirement

Despite our increased longevity, more and more people are retiring early. In some cases this may be a long-planned voluntary arrangement, but during recession years there is always an increase in the number of employees forced into compulsory early retirement (or late redundancy). From the pensions point of view the problem is twofold. First, the number of years of pensionable service – the number of years that count towards your pension – is reduced. Second, the number of years you will draw your pension is increased, so a smaller-than-expected pot of money has to stretch over a longer-than-expected retirement. The two combined can lead to a sharp reduction in the level of the pension offered unless the employer is generous enough (or under enough pressure – from the union, for example) to make good the shortfall.

TAX-EFFICIENT TOP-UPS

The first point to note about AVCs and FSAVCs is that they are approved pension arrangements and almost as tax efficient as company schemes. That means:

- full tax relief on contributions;
- tax-free growth of the fund;
- in certain cases a tax-free cash lump sum at retirement (depending on when you started payments).

As with the main scheme, the pension itself is taxed as income. However, as a general rule only employees can pay into an AVC scheme or an FSAVC plan. The employer usually does not contribute.

The second point to note is that as approved pension arrangements these investment or savings vehicles generally lock your money away until you retire under your main company pension scheme (although FSAVCs tend to be more flexible on this point than AVCs). If you want more flexibility you might consider investing some of your money in ISAs, which offer similar scope for tax savings, although the tax breaks apply in different ways. The use of ISAs in retirement planning is explained later in this chapter.

COMPANY AVCS

An AVC scheme is a company top-up pension set up by the employer or trustees to run in conjunction with the main scheme. However, in most cases the investment and administration of the AVC scheme is sub-contracted to a third party. The majority of equity-based AVC schemes are run by life offices plus a few unit trust groups and institutional fund managers. The building societies tend to run the deposit-style accounts.

Trustees' role

The choice of provider is usually left to the trustees. Research by actuarial consultants indicates that trustees do not always take this particular role very seriously. In contrast, the investment

Ask the trustees what criteria were used to select the AVC provider and how often the scheme is monitored.

management of the main company scheme has a high profile and as a result the trustees, with the help of the scheme adviser, will spend a great deal of time selecting and monitoring the manager. When it comes to the AVC provider, by retirement the best companies can produce funds worth 20 per cent more than the poor performers. Yet many trustees do not go through the same careful selection process as they do for the main scheme fund manager, neither do they monitor the AVC arrangement often enough.

The contract or agreement to make AVC payments is between the employee and the employer, so if you want to check any details you must go to the trustees or pensions manager. Before joining, therefore, you should ask the trustees what criteria were used to select the AVC provider and how often the scheme is monitored. If the trustees are well informed they will have access to the latest surveys on AVC performance; if their provider is not above average over the long term, they should change the company.

It is also important to check how flexible your contributions can be. Ideally you should be able to pay what you like, when you like, within Revenue limits of course. But some pension companies are likely to lock you into regular monthly contributions and if you stop or reduce payments you might be penalised (for details of how providers' charge work, *see* Chapter 1).

Contributions and benefits

Most AVCs operate on a 'money purchase' basis. This means that although the main scheme may provide a pension linked to salary, the AVC scheme is likely to invest the contributions to build up a fund which at retirement is used to buy an annuity from a life office. This annuity provides a guaranteed income for life but the value of the annuity is dependent on the investment returns achieved by the AVC fund and has no link to the value of your final salary. (*See* Chapter 6 on annuities.)

Some AVC schemes – mainly those in the public sector – offer 'added years'. This means that contributions buy extra 'years' in the main scheme where the pension is salary linked. For example, in a 'sixtieths' scheme, where the maximum two-thirds pension is achieved after 40 years, if you estimate you will only have 30 years of pensionable service at retirement you might be able to close the gap by buying several more 'years' through the AVC scheme. The advantage of added years is that the pension you buy has a known value which is linked to the rise in earnings. However, the opportunity to buy added years is becoming less common and even where it is available, the cost can be prohibitive.

FREE-STANDING AVCs

Free-standing AVCs were introduced in October 1987 as part of a government drive to increase pension options. FSAVCs are individual contracts between the employee and the provider. The employer and scheme trustee are not involved and usually do not even need to know about the arrangement unless you are paying very high contributions.

The FSAVC market is dominated by the life assurance companies, although an increasing number of institutional investment managers and unit trust groups are launching products.

Why go for a FSAVC?

At first glance there seems little merit in looking outside the company scheme for a top-up arrangement. Certainly if you are paying less than £50 a month, it will probably be uneconomic to go for an FSAVC because of the high running costs.

The chief selling point of FSAVCs is their investment scope. While most larger company schemes offer an investment choice under their own AVC arrangements, there are many schemes that provide a single AVC option, often a deposit-style account run by a building society, or a 'with-profits' fund run by a life office (*see* page 110 for investment options). FSAVCs, on the other hand, offer a wide choice of funds.

CONTRIBUTION AND BENEFIT LIMITS

One of the confusing things about AVCs and FSAVCs is that they can look so different from the main company scheme that it is tempting to see them as a totally separate investment. Not so. The only time you can pay into an AVC or FSAVC is when you are a member of a company scheme, while the amount you can pay in is dictated by the level of your contributions to the main scheme.

How much can I pay in?

The Inland Revenue rules are quite generous here. You are allowed to pay a total of 15 per cent of your earnings into the main scheme and AVC/FSAVC combined. Since most employees pay about 5 per cent to the main scheme, this leaves up to 10 per cent for the top-up scheme. If you are lucky enough to belong to a 'non-contributory' scheme, where the employer is the only one paying contributions, you can invest the full 15 per cent of earnings into your AVC/FSAVC provided you don't exceed the overall maximum pension of two-thirds final salary. Bear in mind also that AVC/FSAVC contributions can be based on your total taxable earnings from your employer, whereas contributions for the main scheme may be based on basic pay.

Some employees will be caught by the 'earnings cap', introduced by the 1989 Budget, which limits total pension contributions to 15 per cent of £90 600 (for the 1999–2000 tax year). The earnings cap affects employees who joined a new occupational scheme set up after 14 March 1989 and for new members who joined an existing scheme after 1 June 1989.

Over-funding

If you accidentally overfund your scheme, excess contributions will be refunded, less a tax charge.

Tax relief on contributions

The way tax relief is applied to your contributions will depend on which arrangement you opt for. Tax relief on company AVC contributions is provided through the 'net pay arrangement' which means that you get immediate tax relief at your highest rate. Contributions to FSAVCs are paid net of basic rate tax and this is reclaimed from the Inland Revenue by the FSAVC provider. Higher rate tax relief is gained through your end-of-year tax assessment.

What benefits can I take?

The benefits you can take from a company AVC scheme have changed over the past few years and several systems apply, depending on when you started your contributions.

- Where AVC contributions began *before April 8 1987*, the whole fund can be taken in cash provided the total cash taken from AVC and main scheme combined is within Revenue limits. The advantage of taking the AVC in cash is that the pension from the main scheme is not reduced to provide the cash lump sum (a process known as 'commutation').
- *From 17 March 1987* the Revenue restricted the level of salary on which the tax-free cash calculation was based. The ceiling was £100 000, so that the maximum cash taken from AVC and main scheme pension combined was £150 000 (one and a half times the £100 000 salary limit).
- Where contributions to the AVC scheme started *on or after 8 April 1987*, the whole of the fund must be taken in the form of pension, although its value is taken into consideration when the tax-free cash from the main scheme is calculated. The AVC fund itself is used to purchase an annuity from a life office to provide the retirement income. And, of course, those employees affected by the earnings cap will be further restricted on the total amount of pension that can be taken from main scheme and AVC combined.

Since FSAVCs were only introduced in 1987, there is no tax-free cash option with this product.

So far the benefits all relate to pension. It is possible, however, to use part of your AVC allowance to buy additional life assurance. As with personal pension life assurance, effectively the premiums are tax free.

INVESTMENT OPTIONS

The AVC investment options fall into three main categories and mirror the options available under personal pensions which are explained in Chapter 4.

Deposit accounts

AVC deposit accounts are available from building societies and a handful of life assurance companies. They operate in a similar way to ordinary deposit accounts but with the added attraction of tax relief on the contributions and tax-free roll-up of the fund. With a deposit account the nominal value of your capital is guaranteed but its real value above the rate of inflation may not increase or may even decrease if interest rates are low. However, if you are planning to pay AVCs for just a few years before retirement, this is likely to be the safest home for your money. For five years and over, advisers usually recommend an element of equity investment to provide a better real return.

Charges are either deducted before your contribution is invested, or deducted from gross interest paid. The two methods are not readily comparable since in the case of the former the interest is being applied to a reduced contribution, while the latter assumes the full contribution is invested but a reduced interest rate applies.

With-profits

With-profits funds are the traditional home for low- to medium-risk investors. However, you may also be offered a guaranteed fund which protects you against stockmarket falls (*see* page 55).

Unit-linked/unit trust

Under a unit-linked or unit trust AVC/FSAVC your contributions buy units in a fund of your choice and the performance of these units mirrors the performance of the underlying fund. Few of these funds offer any guarantees and performance can be volatile. However, investment experts argue that there is far more scope for capital growth with, for example, a managed unit-linked fund, which invests in a range of the provider's main funds, than with a with-profits fund (*see* page 49).

FLEXIBILITY

Do check your FSAVC plan for flexibility and portability. You can only contribute to one of these plans in any tax year, so do take advice before you make your choice. You should be able to stop and start contributions, and increase or decrease payments without any financial penalty. If you change jobs you should be able to make the plan paid up (terminate payments completely) or adapt it to your new employment circumstances. For example, if you become self-employed for a period, then the provider should let you continue to make your contributions to a personal pension plan without charging for the administration involved in the change-over.

If you are in doubt over your long-term employment plans follow the golden rule of flexibility and pay for your advice by fees or single premium (one-off) contributions, rather than commit yourself to a regular premium plan, which may give rise to hefty penalties if you are unable to keep up contributions for some reason.

INDIVIDUAL SAVINGS ACCOUNTS

Individual savings accounts (ISAs) were introduced in April 1999 and replace tax-exempt special savings accounts (TESSAs), which were tax-free deposit accounts, and personal equity plans (PEPs). Under the rules you can invest £5000 per annum in an ISA (£7000 in 1999–2000), including up to £1000 in deposits (£3000 in 1999–2000); and £1000 in life assurance funds.

ISAs make excellent long-term, flexible savings vehicles.

One of the important features of the ISA is that many will comply with government benchmarks (CAT-marks) for low charges, easy access, and fair terms. These will not offer any guarantee of performance, but at least you know you will not be overcharged or stuck with an investment that imposes penalties if you want to switch to another provider. Moreover, the Government proposes to allow transfers from ISAs into pensions.

ISAs are broadly as tax efficient as AVCs and FSAVCs and make excellent long-term, flexible savings vehicles. Indeed for some investors ISAs will appear more attractive than AVCs/FSAVCs.

With both AVCs and ISAs the fund rolls up free of Capital Gains Tax and virtually free of Income Tax. However, in other respects the tax treatment differs. AVCs qualify for full tax relief on contributions, but apart from some earlier plans all the fund must be used to buy an annuity at retirement to provide a taxable income. With an ISA there is no tax relief on contributions, but the fund can be withdrawn tax free at any time and does not have to be used to buy an annuity. Higher earners in certain company schemes and who have personal pensions are caught by the pensions 'cap', which restricts to £90 600 in 1999–2000 the amount of salary on which pension contributions and, for company schemes, benefits are based. These investors can use ISAs to build up a retirement fund to cover earnings in excess of the cap.

Key points

Do you need a top-up?

To find out if you need to top up your pension through AVCs or FSAVCs consider the following points. Your company pensions manager should be able to help you assess the shortfall, if applicable.

- **If you stay in your current company scheme will you be on target to build up a two-thirds final salary pension?**
- **Have you changed jobs and left pension benefits behind or taken a transfer value to a new scheme? If so how has this affected the value of your future pension?**
- **Have you ever taken a break from pensionable employment, for example unemployment, self-employment, career breaks to continue your education or to raise children?**
- **Do you earn bonuses or overtime that are not taken into account for the company pension scheme?**
- **Is the company pension scheme 'integrated' with the State scheme?**
- **Do you want to retire early?**

Which product is right for you?

If you decide you do need to top up your pension, consider the following points:

- How does the company AVC work? Does it offer 'added years' or a 'money purchase' fund that will be used to buy an annuity?
- Does the employer pay for some or all of the life assurance company's charges?
- Does the company scheme offer the sort of investment option you need? Younger people should invest in a with-profits or managed unit-linked or unit trust fund rather than a deposit-style account.
- Do the trustees monitor the company AVC scheme regularly to check that the performance is good enough? Ask to see details of comparisons with other companies.
- If you want a FSAVC, have you sought independent financial advice to make sure you get the best value in terms of charges and performance?
- Can you stop or reduce contributions whenever you want to without penalty?
- Are you happy in the knowledge that your top-up plan locks away your investment until retirement? If not, consider putting some of your money in an individual savings account (ISA).

9

Special pension schemes for high earners

- Who is affected by the earnings cap?
- Pension options for capped employees
- Funded unapproved schemes
- Unfunded unapproved schemes

Summary

The Government's attitude to tax incentives for private pension provision is that generally this is a Good Thing because the more people are encouraged to save to look after their own financial needs in retirement, the less politicians need worry about struggling to maintain a universal State pension system. However, at a certain level of earnings the tax breaks start to look more like a luxury than a necessity. The Government regards this as a Bad Thing.

As a result, over the past decade or so, the Government has systematically curbed the tax relief available on pension schemes for higher earners, for example by restricting the amount of tax-free cash that could be taken from a pension scheme. But the most severe blow was dealt by the Finance Act 1989, which introduced the 'earnings cap' – a ceiling on the amount of salary that could be taken into consideration when calculating pension contributions and benefits.

WHO IS AFFECTED BY THE EARNINGS CAP?

The earnings cap affects members of company pension schemes set up after the 1989 Budget and members who joined any scheme after 1 June 1989. This means that if you are a high earner planning a job change you will be caught. You may not be capped at present, but the very act of leaving an old scheme and entering a new employer's scheme will trigger the earnings cap rules – although only for future service. The cap cannot be applied retrospectively to restrict pension rights already built up. This means you could end up with part of your pension based on full earnings and part based on the cap limit – a situation that confuses just about everyone, including the Inland Revenue and pension scheme actuaries.

The earnings cap is £90 600 for the 1999–2000 tax year, which means that the maximum pension for those whose entire pension rights are affected will be £60 400 (two-thirds of the cap), while the maximum contributions for the year will be limited to 15 per cent of the cap – £13 590. The cap normally rises in line with retail price inflation.

PENSION OPTIONS FOR CAPPED EMPLOYEES

Employers recognise that senior executives naturally demonstrate a keen interest in the pension benefits associated with their salary package and that these have to be competitive in order to attract and retain the best people. For this reason many employers provide special pension plans for earnings in excess of the cap.

However, there is no legal requirement for employers to provide pension arrangements for employees earning above the cap and some employers take the easy way out and do nothing. They probably hope that high earning employees either will not notice or, if they do, that they will not realise how great their loss is or that there are ways of compensating for this pension shortfall. Other employers avoid any further pension provision for earnings above the cap but may compensate employees in different ways – for example, increased salary, bonuses, company share schemes and other financial benefits.

There are, however, some genuine pension options, although these might not always be suitable. If you are affected by the earnings cap it is wise to seek independent advice from a pensions expert who can help you make an informed decision about your employer's arrangements and, where necessary, suggest improvements. In theory there is no ceiling on the level of pension provided under these 'unapproved' pensions – the only limit is the depth of your employer's pocket.

■ Unapproved pension schemes

The Inland Revenue permits employers to use certain types of 'unapproved' schemes to top up the pension benefits of capped employees. The term 'unapproved' is not intended to be in any way derogatory or to indicate a slightly suspect arrangement. It simply means that although the Revenue recognises these schemes as genuine pension arrangements, it will not grant the usual tax benefits associated with approved schemes.

Unapproved schemes can be either 'funded' or 'unfunded'.

FUNDED UNAPPROVED SCHEMES

The first is a funded unapproved scheme, or, to be precise, a 'funded unapproved retirement benefit scheme' (FURBS). Under a FURBS, the employer sets aside contributions to build up a pension fund for the employee's earnings in excess of the cap. FURBS usually operate on a money purchase basis. This means that rather than providing a salary-linked pension, contributions are invested to build up a fund which could be used at retirement to purchase an annuity to provide extra regular (taxed) income or it can be taken as tax-free cash. No prizes for guessing which is the more popular option. The FURBS member will usually join the main company scheme and receive benefits in the usual way up to the level of the cap.

The fact that the FURBS has an identifiable fund, written in trust for the employee, probably makes it the most secure arrangement for individuals affected by the earnings cap.

Tax treatment

The main difference between standard company schemes and FURBS is that contributions to approved schemes benefit from tax relief, the pension fund grows free of capital gains tax and virtually free of income tax, while the pension itself is taxed as income, although a proportion of the fund can be taken as a tax-free cash lump sum. With a FURBS the employee is taxed on the employer's contributions, which are classed as a benefit in kind. However, the employer can treat these contributions as a trading expense for corporation tax purposes, and to compensate for the additional tax on the employee, the employer can use a 'grossing up' arrangement with the Revenue so the company pays direct the additional tax bill incurred by the employee on the pension contribution.

Under the original rules, employers did not pay National Insurance on their contributions to a FURBS but by April 1999 this exemption had been withdrawn. The FURBS fund is subject to Income and Capital Gains Tax at the basic rate.

As mentioned above, where the fund is used to buy an annuity pension the income is subject to tax. However, the entire benefit can be taken as a tax-free lump sum on retirement. If you do need a regular income it would be better to take the cash and buy a 'purchased life' annuity, as this is paid partially tax-free. The death-in-service lump-sum benefits can be paid under discretionary trust and therefore should be free of Inheritance Tax.

From the employee's point of view this arrangement can be very attractive, provided the employer is prepared to foot the bill. From the employer's point of view the pension provided under the FURBS is much more expensive than the main approved scheme pensions due to the absence of tax reliefs on contributions and the roll-up of the fund, plus the requirement to pay National Insurance on the pension contributions.

This arrangement can be very attractive, provided the employer is prepared to foot the bill.

UNFUNDED UNAPPROVED SCHEMES

The second choice is the 'unfunded unapproved retirement benefit scheme' (some pension buffs use the acronym UURBS, but the pronunciation is rather challenging). In these arrangements your employer does not pay any contributions and there is no fund earmarked for the employee. Instead the pension benefits are paid out of company funds when the employee retires. When this happens the employer receives an allowance against Corporation Tax.

The good news here is that there is no tax liability until you receive the benefits, but when that happens all lump sums and pensions are taxed as earned income. Where the employer decides to buy an annuity for the employee, the purchase price will be taxed, as well as the resulting regular income. Death benefits, as with the FURBS, should be free of Inheritance Tax if paid under a discretionary trust.

Security

While the tax implications of the unfunded route look more favourable during the period the employee earns the right to the benefit, there are important security considerations. For example, what would happen to the employee's pension if the company went into liquidation or was the subject of a hostile take-over? Under these circumstances the main scheme should be safe, since it is established under trust and has a fund that legally is separate from the company assets and earmarked to pay benefits to scheme members and their beneficiaries. However, with the unfunded unapproved scheme there is no identifiable fund, so if the pension rights consist of little more than a verbal promise from the employer, there is a danger that the employee could lose out.

Unfunded unapproved pensions are still in their infancy and until they are more established you should seek professional help and take care to protect your pension rights by setting them out in a legal document.

Key points

If you are likely to be caught by the cap it is important to consider how best to tackle the pension issue.

- Make sure that your pension benefits relating to uncapped salary are topped up to the Inland Revenue maximum (*see* Chapters 7 and 8).
- Consider the importance of security when looking at funded and unfunded unapproved arrangements.
- Examine other options your employer may offer to compensate for loss of pension on capped earnings – for example, bonus payments, approved share option schemes, subsidised company mortgage, extra life assurance.
- Always seek professional advice so that you can make an informed choice and compare the monetary value of different benefits.

10

Pension transfers

- Employers at fault
- How your 'transfer value' is calculated
- The transfer choices
- Cash refund
- Deferred pensions
- Transfer to the new employer
- Transfer to a personal plan
- Early retirement benefits
- Redundancy and pensions
- Fee-based advice

Summary

The transfer of pension benefits from one company scheme to another or from a company scheme to a personal pension is one of the most complex areas of financial planning and a minefield for the unwary. Unfortunately, just about everyone is likely to hit this problem at some point during their working life. Unless you spend a 40-year career with one employer, who maintains the same pension scheme throughout, then you need to be armed with some vital information. Otherwise you could make a very expensive, irreversible mistake.

You will face transfer trouble if:

- you change jobs, leave the old pension scheme and want to join your new employer's scheme;
- you leave your company to become self-employed;
- you are made redundant;
- your employer introduces a new type of scheme after a take-over, merger or privatisation.

EMPLOYERS AT FAULT

In the wake of the personal pension mis-selling scandal you could be forgiven for thinking that the employers are the good guys and the insurance boys are the bad and the ugly. However, this picture is far from accurate. For while we have come a long way in terms of the regulation of transfers to personal pensions, most employers with final salary schemes have not changed their inequitable rules one jot and continue to penalise early leavers. If these were insurance companies and they applied the same rules to, say, a with-profits funds, they would be howled out of court for permitting such huge cross subsidies between different categories of members and, worse still, from members back to the employer.

It is important to bear in mind that the employer's contribution to a final salary pension scheme is variable. If the scheme has more assets than liabilities, perhaps because it has saved money over the long term by making transfers and early redundancy payouts, then employers can reduce the amount they pay in on your behalf and even take contribution 'holidays'. So the members' losses are the employers' gains.

Now this would be bad enough if occupational pensions were a form of paternalistic, charitable giving on the part of employers. But they are not. Your pension forms part of your employment contract or benefits rights – often both. Moreover your pension is clearly defined as deferred pay by the European Court of Justice and enshrined as such in European Union law. The fact that inequitable transfers continue unabated is little short of scandalous.

HOW YOUR 'TRANSFER VALUE' IS CALCULATED

This is where you have to bite the bullet. If you belong to a final salary scheme and want to understand the potential pitfalls with transfers, you need to know how the scheme actuary calculates your 'transfer value' – the figure on the cheque the pensions manager hands over to your new scheme. The documents which are supposed to explain your transfer value may well be the worst example of gobbledygook you have ever seen. In the past employers tended to get away with this, but it is no longer regarded as acceptable. If you don't understand your transfer document, return it to the pensions manager and ask for a version in plain English.

Even in English, the whole process remains something of a mystery, but broadly speaking this is how it works. Under a typical final salary scheme your pension builds up at the rate of one-sixtieth of the value of your salary at or near retirement for each year of service. After 40 years you would have the maximum pension permitted by the Inland Revenue, which is two-thirds of final salary (forty-sixtieths). This may be restricted if you are a higher earner.

The scheme actuary has to do some number crunching to convert the number of 'years' you have built up into a monetary value. In this case, the transfer value is the 'cash equivalent' of these benefits. Well, almost equivalent. To come up with the cash equivalent the actuary calculates what your pension would be worth at retirement but is likely to assume a limited rate of annual indexation. The value of the pension at retirement is then 'discounted back' to the present to give the current transfer value.

The theory behind this calculation is that the transfer value should be sufficient, if reinvested at current rates of interest, to produce the same benefit at retirement as the benefits given up under the scheme. The discount rate reflects market conditions at the time the transfer is paid – for example, stockmarket returns and interest rates. The problem is that in using limited indexation (retail price inflation capped at 5 per cent) rather than full earnings inflation in the calculation of the pension at retirement, there may be a shortfall between what your pension is worth if you stay in the scheme and the value of the transfer value offered. The difference between the transfer value and the real or notional value (known in the jargon as the 'past service reserve') is usually absorbed by the scheme. You lose, the scheme wins.

To illustrate this point, suppose you receive your transfer quotation and ask your pensions manager what would happen in theory if you took the cheque today and then asked to be transferred back

> **This shortfall has nothing to do with soaring inflation and everything to do with the calculation method.**

in to the same scheme tomorrow (in practice the scheme rules do not normally permit this). The honest response would be that the cheque will not buy you back the full level of benefits you gave up. It may be cold comfort but at least you now know that this shortfall has nothing to do with soaring inflation and everything to do with the calculation method.

How well padded is your scheme?

There will also be circumstances where the calculation method may be affected by the funding level of the scheme you are leaving. For example, if it is awash with surplus funds the transfer calculation may be more generous than at a time when the scheme is verging on a deficit. If any special conditions apply in your case, seek expert advice and ask whether now is the right time to transfer.

Incompatibility between schemes

To make matters worse, few pension schemes or plans are compatible and in many cases a transfer of benefits might involve schemes set up under different tax regimes. Some sort of compromise is usually reached between the ceding scheme (the old scheme from which you are transferring out) and the accepting scheme, so that neither feels it has lost out financially. This compromise is usually at your expense.

Insurance company schemes

If the pension scheme or plan is run by an insurance company, there may be deductions from your fund to cover sales commissions and administration costs (*see* 'Money purchase company pension transfers' on page 131). These charges are discussed in Chapters 1 and 3.

THE TRANSFER CHOICES

Enough about warnings. Now let's look at the pension transfer choices. For the sake of brevity this section considers the most common case, where an employee in a company scheme changes job.

If you were in the scheme and made contributions for less than two years you may be able to get your own contributions back (not the employer's), less a charge for tax.

After two years:

- You can leave the pension benefit in the former employer's scheme (known as a 'deferred' or 'preserved' pension).
- You can take a transfer of benefits (the 'transfer value') to your new employer's scheme.
- You can take a transfer value to an Inland Revenue-approved private individual plan such as a personal pension – but remember, you will lose out on the guaranteed link to salary and instead the value of your pension will be dictated by volatile investment returns. Do not consider this route unless the two main options above are not appropriate.
- If you are over age 50 you may be able to take early retirement benefits from the scheme. The pension is usually severely reduced if you go early unless there is a voluntary redundancy programme in place that offers enhanced terms.

Each option has its merits and drawbacks and should be considered carefully in the light of your particular circumstances. Here we look at the choices in more detail.

CASH REFUND

Employees who have been contributing to a company pension scheme for less than two years may be entitled to a cash refund of their own contributions, normally without interest. The employer's contributions, made on your behalf, are not refunded and simply fall back into the scheme fund. This means that if the scheme was 'non-contributory' – in other words only the employer paid in to the scheme and there were no employee contributions – you will get nothing back.

If you do qualify for a refund it will be subject to either one or two deductions before you get your hands on the cash. First, the Inland

Revenue levies a tax charge, since your original contributions would have benefited from full tax relief. At the time of writing this was 20 per cent, which is less than the basic or higher rate relief you will have enjoyed on your contributions. You can only hang on to the full tax break if you transfer directly to a new scheme or plan.

The second deduction is made by the Department of Social Security (DSS) to buy you back in to the State Earnings-Related Pension Scheme (SERPS) for the period covered by the company scheme membership. This, of course, only applies where the scheme itself was contracted out of SERPS (*see* Chapters 7 and 16 for more details). Contracted-out schemes pay reduced employee and employer National Insurance contributions since they replace most of the SERPS pension. It is this shortfall in NI contributions that the DSS will claw back to reinstate you in SERPS.

DEFERRED PENSIONS

In this case the pension is 'deferred' or held for you until retirement. Given the fact that most people change jobs between five and seven times during their careers, by the time you are in your 50s you could have several deferred pensions behind you. This can be quite confusing and rather messy from an administrative point of view, but don't be tempted to transfer all your deferred pensions to a personal plan just for the sake of neatness or because you dislike your former employers.

Don't be tempted to transfer all your deferred pensions to a personal plan just for the sake of neatness.

There are many advantages associated with deferred pensions, although much will depend on the generosity of the old scheme both in terms of benefits that are guaranteed and benefits that are discretionary (not guaranteed but paid on a fairly regular basis). For example, a certain amount of annual indexation must be applied to the pension between the date you leave and the date you retire. Guaranteed and discretionary increases to pensions in payment (pensions actually being paid to retired employees) are also an important feature to consider when you assess the value of your deferred pension. Most schemes pay increases of between 3–5 per cent per annum to pensioners, while some pay more. Public sector schemes pay the full rate of retail price inflation on pensions in payment as they do on deferred pensions.

Schemes may also offer good death benefits and pensions for widows and young children. These may continue to apply to the deferred pension, although naturally the benefits will be scaled down in proportion to the number of years of membership in the scheme.

TRANSFER TO THE NEW EMPLOYER

If you exercise this option you may feel you have been cheated out of some of your years of service. Unfortunately the rules on inter-company transfers still favour the employer, and what looks like a sleight of hand on their part is perfectly legal.

The calculation of the transfer value by your original employer's scheme was discussed above. The situation becomes more complicated in an inter-company transfer because there are two schemes involved – the ceding scheme and the receiving scheme. You might think that as you have ten 'years' of pension to transfer from the old scheme this will buy you ten years in the new scheme. So why do you only get credited with five? Part of the reason, as explained, is that the transfer value itself is worth less than the real value of your benefits in the old scheme because it does not take into consideration full earnings inflation. Also, your new salary may be much higher than the salary for your former job so the value of your transfer cannot provide the same number of 'years'. In addition, the new scheme may offer better benefits and again this will be taken into consideration.

The main exception to this method of calculation is in the public sector where the 'transfer club' operates. For employees moving from one public sector scheme to another, the transfer club offers the same number of years in the new scheme as in the old. Simple and very good value – although as a result of widespread and over-generous early retirement pensions many public sector schemes are virtually bankrupt and the rules are likely to change in future.

Despite the anomalies inherent in the system, an inter-company transfer is likely to offer better value than a transfer to a personal pension. You may even be able to improve your position by taking your pension transfer into consideration when discussing the pay and benefits package with your new employer.

Money purchase company pension transfers

A growing number of company schemes in the UK are run on a money purchase basis. To recap, this means that contributions are invested to provide a fund at retirement which is used to purchase an annuity from a life office. The annuity provides the guaranteed income in retirement. There is no automatic link between your pension and your final salary.

Money purchase scheme transfers are easier to understand than final salary transfers because your pension has a clear pounds and pence value that saves all the opaque calculations to convert 'years' under a final salary scheme into a 'cash equivalent'. In theory if you are in a money purchase scheme, when you change jobs your transfer value should be the value of your units or individual fund. This is what happens if you are lucky. However, many money purchase schemes run by insurance companies levy high charges during the early years to cover their own administration charges and the sales commissions paid to advisers. If you pull out of this type of contract before the agreed retirement date you may face a hefty financial penalty. An initial charge may also be imposed by the new money purchase scheme. The better schemes are advised on a fee basis and this is paid for by the employer. In this case there should not be any significant deductions for early withdrawal.

If you want to leave a money purchase scheme, ask your employer or pensions manager to find out if early termination penalties will apply. If this is the case you may be able to continue the plan on an individual basis. However, you should only consider this option if the pension company's charges and performance are competitive and it fits in with your other pension options.

Topping up losses

One final point on inter-company transfers. If you are worried about the loss of pension benefits caused by the transfer, do consider topping up your company pension by paying additional voluntary contributions (AVCs), free-standing AVCs or some other form of tax-efficient investment plan, such as an individual savings account (ISA). (*See* Chapter 7 for topping-up ideas.)

TRANSFER TO A PERSONAL PLAN

Only when the above options have been examined and found wanting should you consider a transfer to a personal plan. There is another option called a buy-out bond which may be slightly better in special circumstances. However, most people transfer to personal pensions – partly because they are more flexible and partly because very few companies sell buy-out bonds. The buy-out bond can only accept the transfer value, whereas it is possible to pay regular or additional single premiums into a personal pension. Furthermore, the buy-out bond cannot be used to contract out of SERPS and can be more restrictive in terms of investment scope.

Personal pensions are discussed in Chapter 3 and the mis-selling issue is discussed below. The important point to note in the context of transfers from occupational schemes is that the personal pension is a money purchase plan so that your benefits, which previously were linked to your salary at or near retirement, would be linked instead to volatile investment returns. The personal pension fund builds up to purchase an annuity at retirement which provides the regular income for life. Annuity rates, which are determined by yields on long-dated gilts, are also pretty volatile. So, in effect, if you switch from a good company scheme to a personal pension you are replacing a rock-solid guarantee with a can of worms. The worms may do very well but they might also turn. Moreover, you may also lose many other guaranteed benefits when you transfer out of a company scheme, for example a high level of life cover and good dependants' pensions.

If you switch from a good company scheme you are replacing a rock-solid guarantee with a can of worms.

Positive aspects of personal pensions

However, there are some positive features of personal pensions just as there are negative features of company schemes. First, you gain control of a tangible asset. Under a company scheme you have pension 'rights' but you would be forgiven for thinking that hard cash looks somehow more solid and secure than an employer's promise to pay a pension in 20 or 30 years' time that is based on a rather obscure calculation only understood by mystics and, possibly, scheme actuaries. Under the 1975 Policyholders Protection Act, in the unlikely event that the insurance company goes bust, up to 90 per cent of your contract is covered by a compensation scheme. (From April 1997 members of company pension schemes are protected by a new compensation scheme established under the Pensions Act 1995.)

Second, you have more control over your investments under a personal pension and the companies selling these plans usually offer a wide range of funds. For the wealthy and adventurous investor it is possible to run the fund yourself or appoint a stockbroker to do the job for you, although this flexible option is usually more expensive than the basic package, which would combine administration and investment management. Self-invested personal pensions are discussed in Chapter 5.

In order to compare your final salary company pension benefits with those offered by a personal pension, your adviser will have to analyse the following:

- Details of the benefits you have built up in the scheme, known as accrued benefits, including the prospective tax-free cash sum available. (The adviser will have to contact the trustees of the previous scheme to obtain full information.)
- Details of the previous scheme's practice on death and disability benefits, and on guaranteed and discretionary inflation proofing.
- Details of early retirement benefits available.
- Details of any additional voluntary contribution (AVC) payments paid in the old scheme and any penalties on transfer.

- Details of the benefits offered for deferred pensioners – those who leave their benefits in the scheme after leaving employment. (Again, it will be necessary to contact the trustees for this information.)
- What the transfer value would be worth in the new scheme.
- A full 'fact-find' on you, the client, including future career prospects, attitude to financial risk and family protection insurance requirements.

Only when all this information is collated can the adviser calculate the rate of investment growth required by the personal pension transfer to match the benefits of the previous or new employers' schemes (known as 'transfer value analysis'). The adviser must then ensure that any quotations from a life office mirror exactly the benefit structure of the previous scheme. For example, if the scheme offers 5 per cent inflation proofing and widow's and children's pensions, the personal pension quotation must do the same. If these factors are excluded, the projected pension from a personal plan will appear artificially inflated.

Also, bear in mind that the pension offered by the company scheme is guaranteed, whereas the personal pension quotation will assume a rate of investment growth which may bear no relation to actual experience. These rates are laid down by the regulators to provide a standard basis for quotation purposes.

Finally, if the decision is made to transfer to a personal pension plan or buy-out bond, the adviser should conduct a detailed analysis of the provider's investment performance and charges. It is important that the plan is free of early withdrawal penalties so that you can move your fund should the provider's performance fail to match up to expectations.

Personal pensions: the mis-selling scandal

Probably the most compelling reason for hesitating to switch to a personal pension is the atrocious track record the insurance industry has built up on poorly advised transfers from occupational schemes to these plans.

Litigation is very expensive and should be regarded as a last resort.

Personal pensions were designed for employees who had no pension provision. They were never intended to be a substitute for an occupational schemes – and this applies to deferred pensions as well. Unfortunately the large lump sums associated with transfers from company schemes – typically running into tens of thousands of pounds – proved a prime target for commission-based salesmen and advisers. New rules preventing further mis-selling of personal pensions have been introduced, but the buyer should still beware.

Transfer victims' compensation

If you were mis-sold a personal pension and/or advised to transfer your benefits from a company scheme, you should have received compensation by now. The best outcome by far is to be reinstated fully in your pension scheme for the opt-out period. Where reinstatement is not possible then you are likely to be offered a top-up to your personal pension.

Investors who bought a good-quality plan can regard this as a reasonable second best, provided the level of top-up is adequate. Where large sums are involved, you could ask a firm of pension specialists to check the figure for you (*see* the end of this chapter for contacts and Chapter 1 for tips on how to find a good adviser). However, if you were sold a plan that combines high charges with poor performance, putting in more money only adds insult to injury and you may wish to contest this offer.

Do bear in mind that litigation is very expensive and should be regarded as a last resort. Several trade unions are backing pension transfer cases, so check if yours will provide financial assistance.

EARLY RETIREMENT BENEFITS

If at the time you leave the company you are aged over 50 you should be told about the terms on which you could take an early retirement pension. The main point to consider is the need for income and whether this is worth the price of a (typically) much reduced company pension. You may also consider whether you need greater flexibility over the timing and the level of the pension payments, in which case a transfer to an income drawdown plan may be appropriate, provided you have other sources of income and your pension fund is sufficiently large to bear the regular costs.

REDUNDANCY AND PENSIONS

Pension choices for the redundant are similar to those facing job-changers, but with one major difference – the newly redundant usually have not lined up the next career move and may need to wait several years before their future plans are clear. This is a crucial factor when deciding what to do with your pension rights in the old scheme since you cannot weigh up the pros and cons of, for example, an inter-company pension transfer if you do not know what the next employer's scheme looks like.

Experts recommend that initially you should do nothing unless absolutely forced to take action. This might arise, for example, where your former company closes down and the pension scheme is wound up (terminated), in which case you will have to accept the employer's terms for transfer or do something yourself.

You may also be offered early retirement. During a recession many companies embarking on major redundancy programmes put forward a special pensions deal for volunteers. The most common perk is early retirement without the actuarial reductions that normally apply if you go before the scheme's normal retirement date. This can boost your pension by as much as 20–30 per cent, depending on how far to retirement you have to go.

If you are offered this option make sure you know exactly how the package works. Does it, for example, credit you with the full number of years you would otherwise have worked up to normal retirement date? Does it take full account of any salary increases you would have received during this period? Care should also be taken with the 'golden handshake'. Anything over £30 000 will be taxed at your highest rate, so it may be preferable to have any excess over this amount redirected into your pension scheme if possible.

FEE-BASED ADVICE

Finally, if you are considering or indeed are forced to transfer your benefits out of a company scheme, seek professional advice, preferably on a fee basis. The advice you receive should not be linked to the sale of a product because the right course of action may well be to leave your pension benefits where they are. With the best will in the world, an adviser or company representative who is only or largely remunerated by commission is going to want to make that sale.

Key points

- **Do seek professional advice and expect to pay on a fee basis.**
- **Do get all the facts about your old scheme and your new scheme before deciding what action to take.**
- **Don't consider transferring to a personal pension unless you have explored the possibility of taking a deferred pension or transferring to the new employer's scheme, if applicable.**
- **Do seek independent advice if you need to start a personal plan. Look for flexibility to stop or reduce contributions (without penalty), low costs and good long-term performance.**
- **Don't make a hasty decision if you have been made redundant. Leave your pension in the old scheme until you have found a new job and can decide whether or not to transfer it to the new scheme.**
- **Don't transfer your pension just because you dislike your employer. You are probably doing the company a favour financially if it can get rid of you by paying a transfer value that is worth less than the real value of your benefits.**

Further information

Several organisations provide leaflets on transfers. A good introduction to the subject is *Pension Transfers: How to Decide* published by the National Association of Pension Funds (NAPF). Contact: NAPF, 12–18 Grosvenor Gardens, London SW1W 0DH. Tel: 0171 730 0585. Fax: 0171 730 2595.

If you are unhappy about the pension transfer details from your scheme, write in the first instance to the scheme trustees. If this proves fruitless contact the Occupational Pensions Advisory Service (OPAS), preferably through your local Citizens Advice Bureau (*see* Chapter 19). If the problem lies with an adviser or life assurance company, you should put your complaint in writing to that company. If this does not sort out the matter, write to the relevant regulatory authority, which will be given on the firm's headed paper.

If you have a query about a mis-sold personal pension contact the Financial Services Authority's helpline: 0171 417 7001.

For a list of specialist advisers who can help with an assessment of compensation for a mis-sold pension, telephone the Association of Consulting Actuaries: 0171 248 3163.

11

Troubleshooting: when your company changes hands or the pension scheme is terminated

- Danger signals
- Company insolvency
- Bankruptcy
- When the company changes hands

Summary

Unlike diamonds, pension schemes are not for ever. Situations arise when the sponsoring employer of a scheme may change or it may become necessary to terminate a scheme. These circumstances can at times lead to a fierce battle on the part of the scheme members to retain their valuable rights. Of course not all cases where the scheme is 'wound up' – the legal term used to describe the closing down of a pension scheme – give rise to serious concerns, but nevertheless it is in your interests to understand the process and to know when to take action.

DANGER SIGNALS

The two most common events that can trigger a major change to your pension scheme rights and benefits are company insolvency and a change in the ownership of the employer, whether this is a privatisation, take-over or merger.

COMPANY INSOLVENCY

Figures from the Department of Trade and Industry reveal that typically some 15 000–20 000 companies in the UK go bust each year. Many more hover on the brink, desperate for a cash injection. The 'cash-poor, pension-fund rich' company became a hallmark mark of the recession years. Despite the fact that these pension funds are set up under trust, insolvency investigations revealed that a small but significant minority of employers tapped into the pension assets. Funds also ran low where employer contributions were small and/or investment returns were poor.

Two provisions under the Pensions Act 1995 should help protect scheme members' benefits in these circumstances. The first is a minimum funding requirement (MFR) which is supposed to ensure the employer contributes enough to keep the fund fully solvent and therefore able to meet all its liabilities to its members at any time. The second is a compensation scheme which will pay your benefits if the worst happens and your employer runs off with the loot.

Ironically, it is better from your point of view if your employer commits fraud because that will be covered by the compensation scheme. If the shortfall in the fund is due to poor investment you will not qualify for compensation.

■ The independent trustee is your friend

If your company goes bust the first point to check is that the insolvency practitioner has appointed an independent trustee whose role is to make sure the members are fairly represented. Moreover, where the original trustee board has dispersed, the insolvency practitioner's influence could in theory lead to certain

> **The important point is knowing when to act and when to leave things to the professionals.**

conflicts of interests unless there is an independent trustee to provide a balance of powers. Remember, the insolvency practitioner's main duty is to collect as much money as possible for the creditors – the pension scheme is just one more in a very long queue.

In insolvency cases the scheme itself almost certainly will be closed down. But even where there is no suspicion of fraud, the length of time it takes to sort out your benefits can be unnerving. The important point is knowing when to act and when to leave things to the professionals.

Delays are inevitable

Certain delays in disentangling the pension benefits from the insolvency quagmire are understandable. In order for the scheme to be wound up it is necessary for the assets of the fund to be assembled and turned into cash. This is a complicated procedure, particularly if the fund had direct investment in illiquid assets such as property, where it might take several years to wait for the market to turn in order to get a good price. You may feel anxious to get your money out of the company fund as quickly as possible, but ideally you should wait until all the scheme assets have been collected and your position is clear. If you are considering a transfer of benefits, read Chapter 10 which deals with this complex subject in more detail.

Other delays may relate to the administration of the pension scheme. Records on each member's length of service, salary and transfers into the scheme, for example, could be incomplete and the independent trustee must fill in any gaps before the scheme's liabilities can be fully assessed. One way to help here is to write to the insolvency practitioner or independent trustee to check your personal records are accurate.

If the independent trustee is able to wind up the scheme, annuities and deferred annuities must be bought to provide members' pension income. Annuities pay an income for life, with immediate effect, in return for a lump sum investment (*see* Chapter 6). These would be used for existing pensioners. Under a deferred annuity the life office guarantees to pay the income but it starts on a predetermined future date when you reach retirement age under the old scheme rules. An alternative to a deferred annuity, if you have found another job, is to transfer your pension to your new employer's scheme or to a personal plan (*see* Chapters 3 and 10).

If your scheme is 'in deficit' this means there is not enough money to pay out the full benefits guaranteed. The deficit automatically becomes a debt on the employer, but it does not have the status of a 'preferential' debt and so the independent trustee will have to fight it out with all the other unsecured creditors after the Inland Revenue and those with debentures or mortgages have first taken their share. In these circumstances the pensions in payment have priority and all other benefits may be reduced on a pro-rata basis.

Continued life assurance

A vulnerable period during any transitional arrangement is when the life assurance elements of your pensions package are no longer looked after by the old scheme and have yet to be covered under a new arrangement. It is the trustees' duty to make sure proper cover is in place or, if the scheme is to be wound up completely and no new scheme established (as happens in the case of insolvency, for example), then the trustees should notify scheme members in plenty of time for them to take out individual life assurance policies to replace these important family protection benefits.

BANKRUPTCY

The recession has done little to improve official bankruptcy figures which have risen steadily in recent years as thousands of individuals face financial ruin. In this situation you might feel that your retirement provision at least is protected securely through your pension. But some pension specialists believe that the law surrounding pension rights in bankruptcy is hazy and that in certain cases the official receiver (the liquidator) or the trustee in bankruptcy can gain access to your pension fund. Frankly, these cases are very few and far between and are unlikely to affect you if

Next to your family home, your pension fund is likely to be your most valuable possession.

you have been sensible and honest in making your pension contributions in the period leading up to bankruptcy. Moreover, the Government is taking steps to protect all pension funds in the event of bankruptcy.

What happens next?

If you are declared bankrupt, an official receiver or trustee in bankruptcy is appointed to investigate your financial affairs. According to the Department of Trade and Industry (DTI): 'bankruptcy will almost certainly involve the closure of any business you run and the dismissal of your employees. You will have to give up any possessions of value and your interest in your house.' The official receiver will take control of your assets. Either the official receiver or the trustee in bankruptcy will dispose of these assets to pay your creditors. Perhaps most devastating of all, your family home could be sold to pay off your debts. Bankruptcy generally lasts for three years and then the debt is discharged.

Next to your family home, your pension fund is likely to be your most valuable possession. At present, under the Insolvency Act pensions are classed as assets and can, in theory, be used to help pay the bankrupt's debts, although in practice this is very rare. The treatment of your pension will depend, however, on whether you have actually retired (and therefore have a tangible asset) or you are still working and only have 'future rights' to the benefits. By law, employees with personal pensions cannot gain access to their funds until at least age 50. In most occupational schemes they must wait until company pension age – usually between 60 and 65.

Once you start receiving your pension it becomes an asset. For this reason, if you are close to retirement and fear bankruptcy you should consider taking all your fund as income and not taking part of it as tax-free cash (a process known as commutation). Although the trustee in bankruptcy does not automatically take possession of the lump sum, notice can be served on the bankrupt so that the lump sum becomes the property of the trustee. The bankrupt must notify the trustee in bankruptcy within 21 days of receipt of the lump sum.

Loss of pension income

In theory the trustee also can gain access to your income from the occupational scheme. This is achieved by applying to the courts for an income-payments order under the Insolvency Act, under which part of the pension payments are redirected to the trustee in bankruptcy. However, the court will always assess your needs and will not reduce the pension to an amount upon which it would be difficult to live. But no doubt the court's view will be somewhat less generous than your own.

With a personal pension you could face problems if you are over 50 but still working. It is possible for an individual to start taking the benefits from a personal pension plan from age 50, and since the trustee in bankruptcy 'stands in the shoes' of the bankrupt, in theory the trustee can also gain access to the benefits. However, the chances of this happening are extremely remote.

Those with deferred pensions and who are already receiving their pensions should also check their position. Rather worryingly the Social Security Act 1973 states that 'scheme rules can permit forfeiture of "short service" [deferred] benefits when an individual becomes bankrupt'. However, experts reckon that the vast majority of schemes include a Catch-22 clause in the trust deed to get round this ominous threat. The clause allows the trustees to change your 'right' to a benefit into a 'discretion'. In other words it is no longer your right to receive the pension but a voluntary decision on the part of the scheme trustees. Once the benefits can only be paid by the discretion of the trustees, the pension is no longer an asset and cannot be seized by the liquidators.

The Green Paper on pensions published in December 1998 indicated that similar rights would be extended to personal pensions to provide the same level of protection as company schemes.

Avoid temptation

So far, it would appear that bankrupts' pensions are safe. But there are cases where the law will direct its wrath upon them. For example, where a company or individual on the brink of bankruptcy pays large contributions into a pension scheme in a blatant attempt to shelter assets from creditors, the trustee in bankruptcy would have a strong case for trying to gain access to the funds. Even so the law is rather unclear. Part of the problem here lies in the fact that the money is not being passed on to a third party but is being set aside for the bankrupt.

WHEN THE COMPANY CHANGES HANDS

Privatisation

Employees moving from the public to the private sector may be justifiably anxious about their pension benefits. But although individuals have little say in the outcome of major events like privatisations, there have been several successful pressure groups that have won a better deal for scheme members than the original Government proposals.

When you examine the benefits offered by the new private company scheme it is worth bearing in mind several factors. Public sector schemes are particularly generous in the annual increases awarded to pensions in payment (the actual pensions being paid) and to ex-members with deferred pensions. In most cases the increases match full retail price inflation rather than the lower statutory limit of a maximum of 5 per cent that applies in private sector schemes. Although the national and local Government approach is to ensure 'comparable' pensions are offered in newly privatised industries, due to the cost involved there may be some changes and fewer absolute guarantees once the company is privatised. Watch out for vague promises that members' pension rights will continue in the new scheme and ask for a written statement of the new employer's intent at the earliest possible date. Also, assuming you have a choice, take advice before you transfer a pension built up under a national scheme to the new private employer's scheme.

Take-overs and mergers

Ask for a written statement of the new employer's intent at the earliest possible date.

If the organisation you work for changes hands, no doubt your first concern will be job security. Fortunately in most cases you can be confident that the law will protect your rights under your employment contract. What it may not protect, however, is your pension package. This includes your life cover and, in some cases, disability insurance as well.

The security of your pension package will depend partly on your employer's corporate structure and partly on the method used to change ownership. In a classic take-over it is the ownership of the shares that changes, not the employer. In this situation you are still employed by the same company and your entire employment and benefits package remains intact. But problems may arise when your employer sells the business as an asset – usually as a going concern. This is where you are likely to come across 'transfer of undertakings (protection of employment)' (TUPE) regulations. A High Court ruling confirmed that TUPE does not require the purchaser of a business to give transferring employees pension rights equivalent to those previously provided. Which is odd when you consider that under European law, pensions are classed as part of pay.

In fact TUPE appears to let your new employer off the hook altogether. Your employment rights are safe but your pensions package remains with your old employer unless your new employer is prepared to offer you a deal. This deal does not have to match your current package and if – for example in the case of a small acquiring company – there is no pension scheme, the new employer is under no obligation to set one up. In these situations publicity is your best friend. Loss of pension rights is headline news these days and not very good PR for either the selling or acquiring company. In the case of larger companies, the union or an employee pressure group may be able to use publicity to influence the outcome.

If you are employed by a partnership or sole trader, clearly there are no shares to exchange. Instead your firm may be merged with another or the sole trader may sell the business to someone else. In these cases TUPE applies, so once again your contract of employment is secure but not your pensions package.

Troubleshooting

A lot of employees' anxiety during a change of ownership is due to poor communications. Trustees and employers are getting better at keeping scheme members up to date with developments, but do make sure you have a clear, written statement of intent on the following points:

- The level of your new employer's contributions. Do they match the old rate?
- The level of benefits, including the pension itself, death-in-service benefits (lump sum and dependants' pensions) and disability pensions.
- Annual increases to deferred pensions and pensions in payment.
- Discretionary benefits. These are not guaranteed but are paid on a regular basis – for example, extra annual pension increases.

Be particularly careful to check your disability benefits. In some cases these are provided under insurance arrangements and are not part of the pensions package, in which case they should form part of your contract of employment. However, many pension schemes provide early retirement on the grounds of ill health and in this case your disability benefits do form part of the pensions package, so they could be threatened by the TUPE rules.

You might also inadvertently suffer if there is a sizeable fund surplus – that is, where the actuaries calculate there is an excess of funds over those needed to meet liabilities. Often these surpluses are used to pay for a redundancy and early retirement programme as part of the transfer of ownership, but if the fund is run down too much it could adversely affect the remaining members.

Finally, if it looks like the change in ownership may lead to the complete termination of the old scheme, the trustees will be responsible for buying out the members' pension rights in the form of annuities. Annuities are sold by insurance companies and in exchange for a lump-sum investment they guarantee to pay you an income for life either immediately (in the case of existing pensioners) or from your future retirement date (if you are still working).

The main point to check here is that you are getting the same level of benefits from the annuity as was promised by the original scheme.

Key points

- Find out at the earliest possible date the details of any changes to your scheme.
- Make sure any promises given by the new employers are put in writing. If in doubt, get the document checked by a pensions lawyer to see if there are any inconsistencies or if there is a shortfall in benefits compared with the old scheme. (It will be easier and cheaper to do this through the trade union on a collective basis than individually.)
- Keep in touch with the trustees or, if the scheme is insolvent, the official receiver or trustee in bankruptcy.
- Make sure that your records are up to date.
- Expect some delays as the assets are examined and realised.
- If you are concerned that the law is being broken or a mistake in your benefits has been made, contact a pensions lawyer or the Occupational Pensions Advisory Service (*see* Appendix 1).

12

Executive pension plans

- How EPPs work
- Contributions
- Pension benefits
- Investment and other features
- Choice of provider

Summary

Senior executives often belong to a fast-stream version of the main company pension scheme that builds up the pension more quickly and provides better benefits all round. But executives and directors can also be provided for through an entirely separate insurance arrangement known as an executive pension plan or EPP. EPPs, although providing a pension linked to final salary, actually have more in common with personal pensions than standard company schemes.

In the past, EPPs have been popular, but today most advisers reckon that personal pensions, and particularly self-invested personal pensions (*see* Chapter 5) offer a package that is just as good and far simpler. Nevertheless, there are still some people for whom the EPP offers greater flexibility on contributions and possibly better and/or more flexible benefits, particularly as you can use an EPP in conjunction with the main company scheme (which is not possible with a personal pension). So, for example, you could use an EPP to take contributions based on overtime and bonuses and then take the benefits from the plan as part of your early retirement income. You could start to draw benefits from your main company scheme at a later date. However, unlike SIPPs and the small business schemes discussed in the next chapter, you cannot usually separate the administration and investment under an EPP, which means you are stuck with just one company's funds (unless there are external fund links – *see* Chapter 4).

HOW EPPs WORK

Executive pension plans are occupational schemes designed for individual or small groups of senior executives and directors. As such they offer all the usual benefits of company pensions and can be particularly attractive tax-planning vehicles. EPPs were introduced by the Finance Act 1970 and proved popular during that decade. Today EPPs face tough competition from personal pensions, which are simpler to operate although not so flexible for tax-planning purposes.

Anyone considering an EPP should be aware of the complex tax regulations that govern these plans and be sure to get independent expert advice. The overly enthusiastic use of EPPs' tax efficiency by high earners in small companies has attracted the attention of the Inland Revenue on more than one occasion. A recent Revenue crackdown restricted the way these plans can be used to accept extremely high employer contributions in years of profit to reduce the corporation tax bill.

Tax benefits

The tax benefits of an EPP include:

- Full Corporation Tax relief is given on the employer's contribution.
- Full Income Tax relief is given on the employee's contribution.
- The pension fund itself grows virtually free of tax.
- Death-in-service benefits of up to four times salary can be paid to the member's beneficiaries. Where the plan is written in trust this benefit falls outside the scope of Inheritance Tax (IHT).
- Part – and in certain circumstances all – of the fund can be taken as tax-free cash. (This is because the tax-free cash is calculated as a proportion of the final salary and not as a proportion of the fund accumulated at retirement.)
- Spouse and dependants' benefits are automatically provided.
- The pension, which can be taken between age 60 and 75, is taxed as income.

CONTRIBUTIONS

EPPs come from the same stable as small self-administered schemes (SSASs), which are used by small businesses, particularly family concerns (*see* Chapter 13). However, EPP contributions are usually invested entirely in insurance company funds, whereas SSASs can use external fund, managers and invest in a much broader range of assets. (To make matters more complicated, there is also a 'hybrid' SSAS – a cross between an EPP and SSAS – which permits free investment choice once a minimum contribution has been paid into the insurance fund.)

Although the pension is linked to final salary, contributions under an EPP are invested on a money purchase basis and grow in an investment fund that is earmarked for the individual employee. Under most money purchase plans the employee and employer contributions are limited to a certain percentage of annual salary. However, under an EPP while the employee is restricted to a contribution of 15 per cent of salary, until September 1994 there were virtually no restrictions on employer contributions. This was because the level of contribution was based on the projected maximum benefits at retirement and the Revenue permits employers to vary contributions according to annual profit. For this reason, until recently it was possible to justify employer contributions of over 100 per cent of salary for a member in his or her early 20s.

In the past some directors took advantage of this anomaly and channelled huge chunks of company profits into their plans to avoid higher rates of Corporation Tax and National Insurance contributions. This was particularly popular back in the 1970s when Corporation Tax for small businesses was 42 per cent, compared with the current rate of 33 per cent (24 per cent for smaller companies). Executives could also give up part of their salary and get their employer to channel it into their pension. This process, known as 'salary sacrifice', means the chunk of salary redirected to the pension plan is free of Income Tax and National Insurance.

Due to a loophole in the Social Security Act 1973, young employees who changed jobs could leave the company pension scheme and take the whole of their pension benefit with them,

It is essential that you and your employer take great care to meet the Inland Revenue rules.

despite the fact that it was effectively overfunded in relation to the period of service. It came as no surprise when in 1992 the Revenue announced measures to restrict these excessive contributions. The new rules, which came into effect on 1 September 1994, cut maximum contributions paid by employers on behalf of younger employees from over 100 per cent to about 25 per cent of salary.

It has to be said that the new contribution rules, and in particular the transitional rules for EPPs already in force, are extremely complicated and it is essential that you and your employer take great care to meet the Inland Revenue rules. Given the rather ragged reputation of these plans as tax-avoidance vehicles, the Revenue will be keeping a close watch on future contributions.

PENSION BENEFITS

The maximum pension of two-thirds final salary for new members joining on or after 17 March 1987 can be calculated on one of two bases:

- salary in any one of the five years preceding retirement;
- the average salary over three or more consecutive years ending not earlier than ten years before retirement.

Only the second definition can be used for controlling directors (a director who owns 20 per cent or more of the company) and those earning over £100 000 per annum. This is to stop members hiking up their salaries in the last three years in order to boost their pensions. You can achieve an Inland Revenue maximum two-thirds final salary pension after 20 years' service and if you joined before 17 March 1987 you can secure this after just ten years.

A further set of rules applies to plans established between March 1987 and March 1989, which restricts maximum salary for pension purposes to £100 000, with a maximum tax-free cash limit of £150 000.

To complicate things even further, some employees will be caught by the 'earnings cap', which was introduced in the 1989 Budget to reduce the contributions and pensions of high earners. The cap imposes a maximum salary of £90 600 for the 1999–2000 tax year that can be taken into account for pension purposes (*see* Chapter 9). The cap affects employees who joined a new occupational scheme set up after 14 March 1989 and for new members who joined an existing scheme after 1 June 1989. The pension itself is arranged through the purchase of an annuity from a life office, although a recent rule change now allows you to keep your fund fully invested in retirement up to age 75. For full details on annuities and 'income drawdown' plans, *see* Chapter 6.

■ Death benefits

Under Revenue rules the EPP can provide up to four times salary on death in service and this may be arranged either through a separate premium to pay for term assurance or by deducting a small amount from the investment fund on a monthly basis to cover this element. On top of the lump-sum death-in-service benefit, EPPs can also provide a spouse's pension of up to two-thirds the member's maximum prospective pension. In addition you might be able to arrange for a refund of the member's contributions as a lump sum.

■ Contracting out of SERPS

EPPs can be used to contract out of the State Earnings-Related Pension Scheme (SERPS) but advisers usually recommend that an appropriate personal pension is used for this purpose, leaving the EPP to provide benefits on top of this plan.

INVESTMENT AND OTHER FEATURES

Since the majority of EPPs are run by insurance companies, the investment choice is similar to that of personal pensions. This topic is discussed in Chapter 4. The main choices are deposit, with-profits, unitised with-profits, unit-linked, unit trust, investment trust and guaranteed funds.

Many pension companies offer a loan facility for EPP clients, although if you want to use the pension fund for business expansion it is worth considering a small self-administered scheme (SSAS – *see* Chapter 13). Under a SSAS it is possible to arrange a loanback of up to 25 per cent of the pension fund in the first two years (excluding transfers in), after which the limit is 50 per cent of the fund (including transfers in). The most popular use of a loanback is the purchase of business property.

CHOICE OF PROVIDER

The executive pension plan market is dominated by the life offices. As with any insurance product the factors you should consider are the financial strength of the provider, the consistency of the performance track record, the level of charges deducted from your premiums before investment and the flexibility of the contract.

On this last point, as with personal pensions, it is important to retain as much flexibility as you can on the amount invested and frequency of contributions. For example, on a regular premium contract (either monthly or annual), if you retire earlier than the date selected at the outset you may face a hefty penalty. However, if you select an early retirement date, check what proportion of your contributions is lost in management charges, since some providers deduct proportionately more on shorter term contracts. The better designed products do not penalise on early retirement or termination. Nor do they include heavy up-front charges to cover the cost of the adviser's commission. Where commission is paid the amount should be fully disclosed and agreed with you in advance. (*See* Chapter 1 on fees and commissions.)

Key points

- **Seek independent fee-based advice to find out if you would be better off with a personal pension or an executive pension plan.**
- **If you go for an EPP, make sure that all the commission is stripped out of the plan. The high contributions possible under EPPs in the past has turned them into a commission-based adviser's dream come true.**

13

Schemes for small businesses

- How they work
- Contributions
- Benefits
- Investment scope
- Choice of SSAS
- Troubleshooting
- One-member SSASs

Summary

Small family businesses struggling to survive the recession could be forgiven for ignoring their pension planning and concentrating on more pressing financial needs. However, with a special type of scheme, unique to the UK, it is possible to provide for directors' pensions while simultaneously using the fund to develop the business. In particular the fund can be used to purchase new business premises and to provide a sizeable loan to the company. These unusual company pensions are known as small self-administered schemes (SSASs) and were introduced in 1973.

HOW THEY WORK

SSASs offer the following benefits to the scheme member and to the business, although it must be stressed that like any Revenue-approved pension scheme, their primary purpose is to provide retirement and death benefits.

Benefits for members:

- The pension is based on remuneration, including benefits in kind, averaged over three or more consecutive years, where the last year ends within ten years of retirement. This definition applies to controlling directors – that is, directors who, together with family associates, own 20 per cent or more of the business.
- The pension, which is worth up to two-thirds of final salary (restricted for some higher earners), is taxed as income.
- The annuity purchase, to provide the member's pension, can be made at any time up to age 75.
- Death-before-retirement benefits are included up to four times annual remuneration.
- A balance of five years' pension payments may be paid as a tax-free lump sum on death after retirement.
- Spouse and dependants' benefits may be included.
- A substantial tax-free lump sum is available on retirement (broadly up to one and a half times final remuneration, date of entry into scheme, number of years in the scheme and the size of fund accumulated).

Benefits for your business:

- The directors who are members can control the scheme and the investment, subject to Revenue rules.
- The directors also decide the level and timing of the contributions, again within Revenue limits.
- Contributions are tax deductible and there is no tax on the investment income or capital gains of the fund.

- The pension fund can be used to purchase commercial or industrial property on commercial terms. The property can be leased back to the company, again on commercial or 'open-market' terms.
- The pension fund can be used to provide a loanback to the company, again on commercial terms.
- The pension fund can be used to buy shares in the company.

Scheme rules

SSASs are extremely tax efficient and offer considerable investment scope. But these schemes are complex and, due to several major changes over the past few years, they require expert help to ensure the company complies with Inland Revenue and Department of Social Security (DSS) regulations. Non-compliance could lead to loss of tax approval.

SSASs are extremely tax efficient and offer considerable investment scope.

Membership of the scheme, which is normally restricted to a maximum of 12, can be extended to any employee, but is generally limited to directors of the company. This makes sense if the fund is going to be used for commercial purposes since the agreement of all members is essential, particularly where self-investment (investing part of the pension fund in your own company) is concerned.

Eligibility and legal requirements

To set up an SSAS your company must be taxed as a trading company. Directors of investment companies cannot establish this type of scheme. The company's memorandum and articles must allow the establishment of a pension scheme for directors and permit directors to vote on a contract in which they have an interest.

The term 'self-administered' relates to a portfolio of investments held in a trust fund to provide retirement and death benefits for the members and their families. The scheme is established by a trust deed. The trustees are chosen by the directors of the company and usually include all the members of the scheme. They can select and control the scheme's investments or appoint a professional adviser to manage the fund. There also has to be a 'pensioneer' trustee, approved by the Inland Revenue, to ensure the scheme is administered in accordance with Revenue rules and to ensure there is no improper termination of the trust (*see* 'Further information' on page 171). If the company ceases trading the pension scheme assets should be safe from creditors where they are held in the trust fund, again provided there was no improper action (*see* 'Troubleshooting' on page 169).

CONTRIBUTIONS

Until recently the Inland Revenue did not impose a specific limit on employer contributions to an SSAS. Instead the contribution was based on the projected final salary at retirement. This flexibility was particularly useful during years of profit when high pension contributions could be paid to offset Corporation Tax.

For all schemes set up on or after 1 June 1996, new rules apply which limit employers' contributions to roughly 70 per cent of salary (less for younger members and more for older members). Previously employers could pay in 100 per cent of salary and this meant that younger members who left employment with the company could leave with a pension fund transfer that far exceeded what was relevant to their period of service. The new rules do not restrict the overall level of benefits you can take on retirement, they simply aim to slow down the rate at which a younger member's fund builds up. Existing schemes must comply with the new rules by June 2001.

As a type of occupational scheme approved by the Inland Revenue, the employer's contributions are tax deductible and the employee's contributions, if applicable, attract tax relief at the highest marginal rate. Where the employee does pay contributions these are limited to a maximum of 15 per cent of salary. However, advisers usually recommend that the scheme is funded solely through employer contributions since this reduces the overall

National Insurance bill. If the members first receive the value of the pension contributions as salary it would be necessary to pay employer and employee NI contributions.

Bear in mind that the company's contributions will only be given tax relief in the trading year in which they are paid. There can be no backdating.

BENEFITS

Other attractions of SSASs include virtually tax-free growth of the fund, a tax-free sum of up to four times annual salary on death before retirement, and a tax-free cash sum at retirement worth up to one and a half times annual salary. This may be restricted for members caught by the 'earnings cap', which is £90 600 for the 1999–2000 tax year. The cap applies to employees who joined a new occupational scheme set up after 14 March 1989 and for new members who joined an existing scheme after 1 June 1989 (*see* Chapter 9). There are various ways of calculating the final salary figure and these should be discussed with your adviser.

Spouse and dependants' benefits are automatically included under an SSAS (provided there are sufficient funds), while the scheme can also provide a tax-free lump sum on death during retirement. The pension, which is worth up to two-thirds of final salary (again possibly restricted by the earnings cap), is taxed as income. For SSASs set up after March 1987 a maximum pension can be built up after 20 years at the rate of one-thirtieth of final remuneration per annum.

One important point on death benefits is worth mentioning. Clearly a member might die before the scheme has had chance to build up sufficient assets to pay the maximum death benefits permitted by the scheme. To avoid this problem, the trustees often arrange inexpensive term assurance in the early years. These life assurance premiums can be paid in addition to the main pension contributions, are tax deductible and are not treated as a benefit in kind.

The SSAS fund grows on a money purchase basis and therefore its value will depend on the success of the chosen investments and the level of contributions paid. At retirement, the SSAS fund is used to provide an income for life, in the form of an annuity. Retirement normally can be taken at any age between 60 and 75, although it may be possible to retire before age 60 on ill-health grounds. If you leave the company you may be able to take an early retirement pension from age 50. However, in the latter case the Revenue is unlikely to allow you to fund for a maximum pension.

Annuity purchase

One of the attractions of an SSAS is the flexibility over the timing of the annuity purchase. Until recently, the period during which the annuity had to be purchased was restricted to five years, but an amendment in 1994 extended this to any age up to 75. This means that members of SSASs can continue to control the investment of their fund and the annuity payable well into retirement (up to a maximum age of 75) – a facility that is now available under several other pension arrangements. In the same way as with income drawdown, during the period you defer buying your annuity you can draw an income from the pension fund roughly equal to what would have been paid had an annuity been purchased.

Contracting out of SERPS

The SSAS, like other company pension schemes, can be used to allow members to contract out of the State-Earnings Related Pension Scheme (SERPS). However, since this would entail extra regulations and supervision, advisers usually recommend that where it makes sense for you to opt out of SERPS you use an 'appropriate' personal pension (*see* page 37).

INVESTMENT SCOPE

SSASs are extremely tax efficient and offer considerable investment scope. The directors of the company, who are members and trustees of the scheme, can select and control the investment portfolio themselves or appoint an investment manager to run the fund. However, trustees cannot buy an investment from or sell an investment to a member of the scheme or to an associated family member. Nor can they carry out transactions with associated companies.

Permitted investments

Permitted investments include quoted stocks and shares, pooled investments such as unit and investment trusts, cash funds, foreign currency, commercial property, traded options, mortgages and loans. Occasionally it may be possible to invest in mixed commercial/residential properties, but normally residential property is not permitted. Cash is usually held by banks and building societies (which can pay interest gross).

Property

Property is of particular interest to small companies, many of which use their SSAS fund to purchase new business premises that can be let to the company. However, this must be done on an arms-length basis and a commercial rent must be charged. Where property is involved, bear in mind that the pension fund must be sufficiently liquid to provide pensions and related benefits to members. For this reason, the Revenue might forbid you to make a major property purchase if members are within ten years of retirement.

Loans

There are very strict guidelines on loans. Briefly, the fund can lend money to the company on commercial terms provided the loan is for a valid business purpose. In 1991 the Revenue limited loanbacks from the pension fund to the company to 25 per cent of the fund value (excluding any transfers from other schemes) during the first two years of the scheme, and 50 per cent thereafter. Previously the limit had been 50 per cent from the outset. Apart from the loanback facility, it is also possible for trustees to borrow against the scheme's assets, provided Revenue rules are followed.

Self-investment and loanback features are invaluable for smaller companies.

Experts believe that the self-investment and loanback features are invaluable for smaller companies, which usually find it very difficult to get good quality loans, particularly during a recession.

Shares

The fund can buy shares in quoted and unquoted companies. This includes the scheme members' own private company, provided the total value of the shares together with any loans to the company never exceeds 50 per cent of the fund or 25 per cent of the contributions to a scheme during the first two years. In addition, the shares purchased must not represent more than 30 per cent of the voting shares of the company. Expert advice should always be sought with this type of arrangement (*see* 'Self-investment' below).

Sale of assets

In August 1991 the Revenue issued new investment rules for SSASs. In particular, companies must report and submit documentation to the Revenue within 90 days if there is any investment or sale of property and unquoted shares. Reportable transactions also include any loans to connected companies and any borrowing. It is essential that directors are aware of the investment transactions that must be reported, and the time limits, otherwise they could inadvertently lose Revenue approval.

Self-investment

SSAS funds are exempt from the DSS rule that restricts self-investment (investment in the sponsoring employer's company) to 5 per cent so long as the scheme does not contract out of SERPS. In practice most SASSs tend to be highly self-invested. The rules state an SSAS fund can invest in the employer's company provided:

- all members of the scheme are trustees;
- all members agree in writing before the self-investment is transacted. This includes property let to the company.

CHOICE OF SSAS

Under Revenue rules you can only run one SSAS per company which makes the choice of provider extremely important. There are two main options: fully self-administered and 'hybrids'.

Fully self-administered

Fully self-administered schemes generally are offered on a fee basis and are available from solicitors, actuarial consultants and life offices. These organisations and the other professionals they employ provide all the administration and legal requirements, including audited annual accounts, three-yearly actuarial valuations and a pensioneer trustee service. If the trustees appoint a manager to oversee the scheme's investments there will be an extra fee for this service.

Hybrid SSAS

The second option is a 'hybrid' SSAS offered by about 30 insurance companies. Under a hybrid SSAS a significant annual contribution – usually about £5000 in total – must be paid into an insurance fund, while contributions in excess of this can be self-administered. The insurance companies deduct a percentage of contributions paid into their own funds and may also have other fixed charges. These charges cover both investment management and administration of the core services.

Which is right for you?

As a rule of thumb the hybrid SSASs, which charge on a percentage basis, are thought to be more cost effective for annual contributions of less than £10 000 – £12 000. Where contributions exceed this amount, the flat-rate fees charged on fully self-administered SSASs start to look attractive. However, it is possible to improve the clarity of the hybrid scheme if you arrange the scheme through a fee-based adviser and ask for the commission costs to be reinvested. (*See* Chapter 1 for tips on how to pay for advice.)

Of course the decision to go the wholly self-administered route is not just a matter of cost but also depends on the extent to which the directors of the company want to have control over their investments and the need for independent advice.

Schedule D taxpayers

Schedule D taxpayers, such as professional partnerships and practices, cannot set up an SSAS but similar facilities are available through self-invested personal pensions (SIPPs), which are run by several life offices and stockbrokers (*see* Chapter 5).

TROUBLESHOOTING

Due to their exceptional investment scope and the flexibility on contributions, in the past SSASs have come under the scrutiny of the Inland Revenue. The Revenue was concerned that some schemes were established for tax evasion and not for their primary purpose to provide pensions for scheme members and their dependants. Moreover, several years ago an investigation by the National Audit Office revealed an untoward number of schemes that had simply ignored the basic investment rules and were guilty of overfunding, excessive borrowing, paying excessive contributions (to avoid tax) and generally investing in unsuitable assets.

Apart from the restriction on employer contributions, in 1994 the Revenue also clamped down on another abuse whereby some SSASs took advantage of tax reliefs on contributions and then engineered loss of Revenue approval in order to get their hands on the funds. Since November 1994 the Revenue has imposed a special 40 per cent tax on the value of the scheme's funds at the time the scheme loses approval.

In the light of the Revenue's zeal to prevent further abuse of SSASs, and given the complexity of the regulations governing these arrangements, there is only one golden rule to bear in mind: it is essential to get professional independent advice.

ONE-MEMBER SSASs

Although SSASs are usually associated with small family businesses, they can be used by directors of larger companies to build up substantial funds which they can invest in a very wide range of assets. The schemes are also widely used by pop stars, professional footballers and other wealthy individuals with non-standard career patterns.

SSASs are ideal for the peripatetic director who, at 45, does not expect to be with the same company at 65 and therefore prefers to have their own more portable arrangement rather than join a series of company schemes. 'Company doctors' are another group who tend to use SSASs. These are the people who are hired to sort out a company's ills and move on when the problem is resolved. They may work for a wide range of companies but in practice are employed by their own business, which funds their pension arrangement.

Although the Revenue has banned the very exotic investments that used to be held in some SSAS funds – racehorses, works of art and yachts, among others – there is still scope for the unusual. Experts have seen SSASs holding the members' favourite football club, golf club and bars, as well as copyright to favourite music and racecourses. All of this with tax relief on pension contributions and tax-free growth within the fund.

Although the Revenue has banned the very exotic investments there is still scope for the unusual.

The important point to remember is that where there is only one member, there is no one else to suffer if an investment goes wrong. Where there is more than one member they are usually controlling directors, so if they all decide to use their pension fund to invest in their own company or make an 'adventurous' investment, they must do so with their eyes open.

Key points

- **Remember that the primary purpose of an SSAS is to provide members' pensions, not to invest in your business.**
- **Make sure the investment choice is sensible and suitable. Always consider the scheme's liabilities – funds must be available to pay pensions and other benefits when they fall due.**
- **You must appoint a pensioneer trustee (*see* 'Further information').**
- **Your adviser must be a specialist in this field. SSASs are complicated and the Revenue will scrutinise documentation and contributions to check for compliance.**
- **Consider a fully self-administered scheme if total contributions are over £10–12 000 per annum, since this offers more flexible investment scope and, usually, a clearer charging structure than insurance-based products.**
- **If you go for a 'hybrid' SSAS use a fee-based adviser to set up the scheme so that commission costs are stripped out.**

Further information

In order to set up an SSAS it is necessary to appoint a pensioneer trustee who has certain legal responsibilities to check that the scheme is being run properly and, in the event of closure, that it is wound up in accordance with Revenue regulations. Most consultants and providers who advise on or sell the schemes offer this service. If you want to find out more about the role of the pensioneer trustee contact the Association of Pensioneer Trustees: c/o Fairmount Trustee Services Ltd, Fairmount House, Bull Hill, Leatherhead, Surrey KT22 7AY. APT represents the interests of those who act as pensioneer trustees for small self-administered schemes.

14

Introducing State pensions

- Not one pension, but two
- State pension pitfalls
- Pension age
- Social security framework
- National Insurance
- Which State pension applies to you?
- Government proposals to change the State pension

Summary

The UK has one of the most complex State pension schemes in Europe. It also pays out one of the lowest levels of benefit. Over the next two decades the complexities will increase while the pensions paid will be cut even further.

The Government plans to replace the State-Earnings Related Pension Scheme (SERPS) with a flat-rate benefit and to encourage – or force if necessary – those who earn over about £9000 into private schemes and plans. (*See* page 181 for details of the pensions Green Paper, published in December 1998.)

Meanwhile the Department of Social Security (DSS) has added to the general confusion by underpaying SERPS benefit to an estimated 400 000 pensioners following serious teething problems with the new computer for the National Insurance Recording System (NIRS2). Each pensioner is due to receive £10 in compensation. In addition the DSS sparked a furore in early 1999 when it revealed that cuts to the SERPS widows' pension, which will halve this benefit for women whose husband dies after 6 April 2000, were not announced in pensions leaflets over the previous decade.

Moreover, the married couple's income tax allowance will disappear for those who retire after 6 April 2000 where neither spouse is aged over 65. In future these couples can expect to pay an extra £500 in tax.

Overall it looks like a real shambles. However, despite the mistakes and complexities, for many people the State pension is an essential component in the overall retirement income package and can be worth up to £180 per week if you have not replaced the earnings-related element with a private scheme or plan.

NOT ONE PENSION, BUT TWO

The State pension breaks down into two main elements – a basic flat-rate pension, known as the old-age pension, and a pension that is linked to the level of your earnings, known as 'additional pension' or SERPS (State Earnings-Related Pension Scheme). Eligibility to both pensions is built up through the compulsory payment of National Insurance (NI) contributions on part of your earnings. The National Insurance system is explained on page 178.

The maximum single person's basic State pension for the 1999–2000 tax year is £66, while the maximum additional or SERPS pension is about £120 per week. From April 1999 the Government proposes to guarantee pensioners a certain minimum level of income through Income Support. This will top up the basic pension to £75 per week for individuals and £116.60 for couples (more for older pensioners). State pensions rise each year in line with retail prices. They are paid gross but taxed as earned income and should be included in the end-of-year tax return.

For those on very low incomes, the 1999 Budget promised that from April 2000 the minimum income guarantee, based on the old-age pension and Income Support, will rise in line with earnings inflation rather than the lower rate of price inflation. At the time of the Budget the minimum income guarantee was worth £75 a week for a single pensioner and £116.60 for a married couple aged between 60 and 74 (more for older pensioners).

Table 14.1 Weekly state pension rates for the 1999–2000 tax year

Single person's pension (Category A)	£66.75 per week
Married woman's pension (Category B)	£39.95 per week
Married couple's pension (Categories A and B combined)	£106.70 per week
SERPS or additional pension (maximum)	£120.00 per week

This chapter provides a general guide to your rights under the State pension system while Chapters 15 and 16 explain in more detail the basic and additional pensions. For those who would like to investigate their pension rights further, the Department of Social Security provides several useful leaflets and addresses.

STATE PENSION PITFALLS

The State pension system works relatively smoothly if you are employed from age 16 up to State pension age, which is 65 for men and rising from 60 to 65 for women (*see* page 177). However, the career pattern of the vast majority of people involves periods in self-employment, periods spent not in paid work (for example, to raise a family), periods in and out of SERPS, and a whole host of other variables. Each event has an impact on the value of your State pension and how it is calculated. The following examples illustrate the most common areas where extra care over State pension rights is necessary:

- *Early retirement* is increasingly common – whether voluntary or compulsory – and has an immediate impact on the level of State pension you can expect to receive. Don't fall into the trap of thinking that you will automatically receive the full rate of pension even if you have worked for 40 years before retiring.

- *Women's State pensions* are particularly complicated, due to a two-tier National Insurance contribution system (which is being phased out) and different associated benefits. Moreover, long periods spent out of paid employment while raising a family or looking after dependent relatives can also create problems. Extra difficulties may arise when the Government phases in the equalisation of pension ages, when the female State pension age will rise over a ten-year period from 60 to 65. The State pension rights of widows and the divorced should also be checked carefully.

- *'Contracted-out' company pension schemes*. Company schemes often are 'contracted out' of Serps. Where this is the case, part of your NI contributions which otherwise would have gone towards your additional pension is redirected into your company scheme. Until April 1997 most schemes guaranteed to at least match SERPS benefits where they are given up. However, after this date this direct matching of State benefits is no longer compulsory.

- *'Integrated' company schemes* are very common. Under this system, the level of pension promised by the company scheme takes into account the basic State pension. Effectively this means that the employer does not provide any pension for earnings up to the lower earnings limit (£66 per week in 1999–2000) or a multiple of this. Low earners and those who do not qualify for a State pension in their own right can end up with a significant gap in pension provision as a result.

PENSION AGE

The official pension age – 65 for men and 60 for women – is the minimum age at which men and women can claim a State pension in the UK. Reaching this age also triggers eligibility to a wide range of benefits, for example free or subsidised use of public transport and other public services.

By the year 2020 the UK will have a common pension age of 65 for both men and women. This move to equal pension ages, first announced by the Government in the November 1993 Budget, will result in a rather complex phasing-in period.

What is clear is that women born after April 1955 will have to wait until age 65 to claim. Older women should check Table 14.2 to find out their proposed retirement date. The phasing-in period will last ten years (2010–2020).

Table 14.2 Examples of new pension ages for women during the equalisation phasing-in period

Date of birth	*Pension age*	*Year to draw pension*
April 1950	60yr 1m	2010
Oct 1950	60yr 7m	2011
April 1951	61yr 1m	2012
Oct 1951	61yr 7m	2013
April 1952	62yr 1m	2014
Oct 1952	62yr 7m	2015
April 1953	63yr 1m	2016
Oct 1953	63yr 7m	2017
April 1954	64yr 1m	2018
Oct 1954	64yr 7m	2019
April 1955	65yr	2020

Source: Department of Social Security White Paper *Equality in State Pension Ages*

SOCIAL SECURITY FRAMEWORK

To understand how your State pension builds up it is helpful to have a little background knowledge. State pensions come under the general heading of social security benefits, which also include benefits paid to people who, for example, are sick, disabled, out of work or on a low income. Most social security benefits are paid for out of the National Insurance Fund, although due to the strain of increased costs of benefits, extra funding is also derived from taxes. The National Insurance Fund is built up from National Insurance contributions levied on earnings and paid by employers, employees and the self-employed. Purists might argue the point but essentially NI contributions can be regarded as another form of direct taxation.

Moreover the NI Fund is not building up cash to pay your benefits. There is not a 'fund' as such. All that happens is that the NI contributions of those in work are 'spent' immediately on the pensions and related benefits of the retired and other claimants.

NATIONAL INSURANCE

National Insurance for employees is levied on what are known as 'band earnings' – earnings between lower and upper limits (known as the lower earnings limit or LEL, and the upper earnings limit or UEL). These are £66 and £500 per week in 1999–2000. The contributions are deducted automatically from an employee's pay packet while the self-employed pay a flat-rate contribution each month to the Department of Social Security and an earnings-related supplement which is assessed annually through the tax return.

There are four classes of NI contributions:

- *Class 1* – paid by employees and employers. Employees earning below the LEL pay no contributions. Those with earnings above the LEL pay contributions on their entire earnings as follows: an initial rate of 2 per cent on earnings up to the LEL and the main rate of 10 per cent on earnings up to the UEL. Employers pay 3–10 per cent on all an employee's earnings including those in excess of the upper earnings limit. Some married women and widows can still pay a reduced rate of contribution – *see* 'The married woman's stamp' on page 179.

- *Class 2* – a flat rate paid by the self-employed.
- *Class 3* – a flat rate of voluntary contribution that may be paid to protect your NI record in order to maintain your right to the State pension.
- *Class 4* – usually paid by the self-employed in addition to Class 2 contributions. Class 4 contributions are paid as a percentage of profits between lower and upper earnings limits.

All of these, with the exception of Class 4 and the married woman's stamp, count towards 'qualifying years' for State pensions, that is a year in which you paid full rate National Insurance contributions for the complete period (*see* Chapter 15).

The married woman's stamp

Before the present contribution system started it was possible for married women and widows to pay a reduced rate of Class 1 contribution, known as the 'married woman's stamp'. Some women who were married or widowed before 5 April 1977 are still paying the reduced rate. All women who started work after that date must pay the full rate. Moreover, the eligibility to pay the reduced rate can be lost in certain circumstances.

The married woman's stamp originally was popular because it meant a much lower deduction from the weekly or monthly pay cheque. But in return women gave up the right to a full State pension in their own name. Instead they have to claim through their spouse's NI contribution record and claim a Category B State pension which is worth about 60 per cent of the full rate (*see* Table 14.1 on page 175).

Before October 1989 there were still significant savings for most women who paid reduced rate contributions. But after the DSS restructured the National Insurance contribution rate bands, many women could switch to the full rate for little or no extra cost while simultaneously starting to build up a right to their own State

> **You need at least ten 'qualifying years' in order to receive the lowest proportion of the basic State pension payable.**

pension. If you earn about £100 per week you will pay virtually the same amount for full rate Class 1 NI contributions as for the reduced rate and therefore should consider switching. If you earn more than this, ask your local DSS whether the benefits you can expect to build up will compensate for the higher contribution costs involved. Remember, as a rule of thumb you need at least ten 'qualifying years' in order to receive the lowest proportion of the basic State pension payable, although benefits under SERPS build up from day one.

■ Switching to the full rate

Married women and widows who pay NI contributions at the reduced rate will have a valid certificate, in most cases held by their employer. This will bear a reference – either CF383, which is a certification of election to pay the reduced rate, or CF380A, which is a certificate of reduced liability. To switch to the full rate you should contact your local DSS and ask for form CF9 and return it together with your certificate. Check your facts carefully to make sure that you will benefit from the change, since once you have made the decision you cannot revert to paying the reduced rate.

■ Continued reduced rate

If you want to continue to pay the reduced rate, bear in mind this right is lost if you spend more than two consecutive years out of employment (or self-employment) or in very low paid employment and therefore not liable to pay NI contributions. This is known as the 'two-year test'. Moreover the right is withdrawn if your marriage ends in divorce or annulment, although widows who remarry can continue to pay the reduced rate.

WHICH STATE PENSION APPLIES TO YOU?

There are four categories of State retirement pension:

- *Categories A and B* (affecting most people) refer to individuals who have built up a right to the pension through their own contributions and those who claim through a spouse's NI contribution record.

- *Category C* is non-contributory and is only payable to men and women who had reached pensionable age by 5 July 1948. There are very few claims still in payment.
- *Category D* pensions are also non-contributory and are paid when you reach 80 and meet certain conditions.

GOVERNMENT PROPOSALS TO CHANGE THE STATE PENSION

In December 1998 the Government published a Green Paper that contained its proposals to overhaul the State pension system and to introduce 'stakeholder' schemes to provide access to a group pension arrangement to more people. The proposals, some of which are expected to take effect from April 2001, include:

- The introduction of a minimum income guarantee for all pensioners from April 1999. The minimum will be achieved by topping up pensions through Income Support to £75 per week for individuals and £116.60 for couples (more for older pensioners).
- The basic or flat old-age pension is to remain. It will not be means-tested at this stage.
- SERPS will be replaced with a State Second Pension (SSP) which is primarily aimed at those who earn less than £9000 per annum. The scheme will eventually become a flat-rate benefit to encourage middle-income earners to opt out and make private pension provision. (The self-employed initially will be excluded from SSP.)
- Bigger National Insurance rebates for those earning £9000–£18 500 to encourage them to opt out of SERPS/SSP into private pensions.
- Those who claim Home Responsibilities Protection (HRP) will receive credits towards the new State Second Pension.
- The introduction of stakeholder plans should ensure people have access to low-cost, flexible pensions.

- Compulsory pension contributions will not be required initially but may be introduced in future, depending on the take-up of stakeholder pensions.
- An annual statement will be sent to all adults that sets out their prospects for a retirement income based on their current State and private pension entitlements.

Key points

- **Despite its complexities the State pension is a valuable benefit and can be worth up to £180 per week if you have not replaced SERPS with a private scheme or plan.**
- **Eligibility to both the basic and earnings-related pensions is built up through the payment of National Insurance contributions.**
- **Several events can reduce your SERPS pension – for example, periods in unemployment, a career break and early retirement.**
- **Some married women may not be paying the full rate of NI and will not be entitled to a basic pension in their own right, but will have to claim a reduced pension based on their husbands' NI contribution records.**
- **The Government plans to abolish SERPS and replace it with a flat-rate benefit for lower earners.**

Further information

The Green Paper, *A new contract for welfare; partnership in pensions*, price £13.25, is available from Stationery Office bookshops.

15

The basic old-age pension

- How a right to the pension builds up
- Home Responsibilities Protection
- Voluntary contributions
- Early retirement
- Late retirement
- Spouse's pensions

Summary

Many people believe, mistakenly, that the basic retirement or 'old-age' pension is a universal flat-rate benefit. In fact the eligibility rules are complex and by no means everyone qualifies. To help you through the maze, this chapter explains how the pension is earned.

If, however, you still find the whole process a mystery (it was not for nothing that the old Department of Health and Social Security was known as the Department of Stealth and Total Obscurity) the most practical step you can take is to get a 'pensions forecast' from the DSS. This will tell you precisely which State pension benefits you are entitled to and will reveal gaps in your provision. Details of this useful service are provided on page 197.

HOW A RIGHT TO THE PENSION BUILDS UP

To get the full weekly rate of the basic pension, worth £66 (in the 1999–2000 tax year), you must have 'qualifying years' for about 90 per cent of your working life. Broadly speaking these are years in which you paid the full rate of National Insurance contribution throughout.

In some cases you will be credited with qualifying years if you are eligible for certain benefits, for example Home Responsibilities Protection (*see* page 185), Child Benefit and Jobseeker's Allowance, among others. Those who do not build up enough qualifying years in their own name may be able to claim a reduced pension based on their spouse's NI contribution record. To get the minimum basic pension payable (about 25 per cent of the full rate) you normally need a minimum of ten qualifying years.

Working life

Normally the DSS regards your 'working life' as 44 years for a woman and 49 for a man, although the figure for both will be 49 years by the year 2020, following a phased increase in the female pension age from 60 to the male pension age of 65 (*see* page 177).

The DSS generally counts your working life from the start of the tax year in which you reached age 16 to the end of the tax year before the one in which you reach State pension age.

Living abroad

Further details on how working and retiring abroad can affect your State pension rights are provided in Chapters 17 and 18. Briefly, if you have lived and worked in Northern Ireland or the Isle of Man, any contributions you have paid there will count towards your UK State pension.

If you have lived and worked in a European Union (EU) country including Gibraltar, or in any country whose social security system is linked to Britain's by a reciprocal agreement (*see* page 220), the social security contributions you paid may help you to meet the eligibility requirements for the basic pension at home. You may also be entitled to a pension from that country. Ask at your local DSS if you think your right to a pension may be affected by any of these arrangements.

HOME RESPONSIBILITIES PROTECTION

Home Responsibilities Protection (HRP), introduced in April 1978, is designed to help maintain State pension rights for people who stay at home to look after young children or dependent relatives. When the pension is calculated, the number of years you received HRP is taken away from the number of qualifying years you would otherwise need for a full pension. HRP credits for National Insurance initially were available only for the basic State pension but in future, under Government proposals, claimants will also receive flat-rate credits to the proposed new State Second Pension, which eventually will replace the State Earnings-Related Pension Scheme.

So who needs HRP? You will need this benefit if the amount of your earnings in a tax year is less than the lower earnings limit – £66 per week in 1999–2000. However, you may not need HRP if you are already getting Incapacity Benefit as you may already be receiving credits towards the State pensions.

Eligibility to HRP

You can get HRP if, throughout the tax year, one of the following applies:

- you were the main person receiving Child Benefit for a child under 16;
- you regularly looked after someone for at least 35 hours a week, who in turn was getting Attendance Allowance (or similar benefit);
- you received Income Support for 48 weeks of the tax year and did not have to be available for work because you were looking after a sick or disabled person at home;
- you have been covered by a combination of these conditions.

Married women and widows cannot get HRP for any years in which they were paying the reduced NI contribution rate (*see* page 179).

How to claim HRP

It is important to remember that in some cases you will automatically receive HRP, while in other cases you must apply. Automatic HRP applies in each of the following cases:

- where you are the main person in receipt of Child Benefit for a child under age 16 for the whole tax year;
- where you receive Income Support for at least 48 weeks in the tax year so that you can look after a sick or disabled person at home.

You need to apply for HRP in the following cases:

- if you are looking after someone who is getting an attendance allowance, or similar benefit;
- if you are covered for the whole tax year, partly by one of the conditions above and partly by another.

VOLUNTARY CONTRIBUTIONS

Voluntary (Class 3) NI contributions can be used to top up full-rate contributions if they fall short. If you have qualifying earnings from Class 1 contributions but not enough to make it a qualifying year, a statement of your NI account will be sent to you between 15 and 18 months after the end of the tax year. This statement will tell you how many Class 3 contributions you need to pay, but before parting with the money you should check if it is worthwhile. For example, if you are likely to have less than ten qualifying years in total you still would not be eligible to the minimum State pension.

You may also be able to pay Class 3 contributions for back years. To find out if you are eligible, ask at your local DSS – but again, check it will be worth the cost.

EARLY RETIREMENT

Your basic State pension depends on several factors, including the number of years you have paid NI contributions and the length of your working life. This means if you stop work early and no longer pay NI contributions this could reduce your State pension. If you are not credited with earnings for the period before retirement you should ask the DSS if you should pay Class 3 voluntary contributions, since this may maintain your right to a full State pension.

It is not possible to claim the State pension before you reach official pension age. For example, a man age 60 would have to wait five years before qualifying and, where his wife intended to claim a spouse's pension based on his NI record, she would also have to wait until his sixty-fifth birthday.

It is not possible to claim the State pension before you reach official pension age.

Some company pension schemes pay what are known as 'bridging pensions' to employees who retire early and are not immediately eligible to the State pension. Bridging pensions are equal to the State pension and are designed to make good the shortfall in total retirement income in the years before State pension age is reached. The bridging pension stops as soon as the State pension is paid.

LATE RETIREMENT

It is possible to defer your State pension (basic, additional and graduated) for up to five years. Provided you defer for at least seven weeks, the value of your pension will increase. The increase or 'increments' and can be earned on each element of your pension, except age addition and additional benefits where you have dependants.

Bear in mind you can only defer your pension once. When payments start or resume you cannot defer it a second time. Neither can the decision be backdated. Moreover, if your spouse receives a pension through your NI record, he or she must also give consent to the deferment.

One final point on this subject, you must be 'ordinarily resident' in the UK to postpone the date you start your State pension, so those who retire abroad generally do not have this option.

If you want to find out more about what happens if you go back to work and defer your State pension, particularly how it affects your company pension payments, contact your local social security and tax offices.

Late retirement and NI contributions

If you work beyond the State pension age, you do not have to pay any more NI contributions, although your employer must continue to pay its share as before.

It is important to inform the DSS about your work plans when it sends you your claim form for retirement pension. The DSS will then send you a certificate of age exemption to give to your employer to let the company know that there is no need to deduct employee NI payments from your salary. The self-employed also stop paying Class 2 and Class 4 contributions if they work beyond State pension age.

If you give up work early or have previous contribution gaps you should find out if you can pay voluntary contributions to protect your pension. Men age 60 or over and not liable to pay contributions should receive NI credits up to age 65. Your local DSS will advise on these points.

SPOUSE'S PENSIONS

If you do not qualify for a basic pension in your own name, you can claim under your spouse's NI contribution record for a pension worth up to a maximum of about 60 per cent of the main single person's rate. The combination of the single person's pension and the spouse's pension form what is generally known as 'the married couple's State pension'. The main point to note about the spouse's Category B pension is that it is not payable until both the wife and the husband reach State pension age and the husband claims his pension.

As a woman, if you do receive a single person's (Category A) State pension in your own right, but it is worth less than the Category B pension, then when your spouse reaches age 65 or retires to claim his pension you will receive a composite pension worth a maximum of the full Category B rate. This composite rate can give you up to the full value of the Category B pension, even if your husband does not have enough qualifying years for the full Category A pension.

It is also possible for a woman claiming a Category B pension to defer payment and earn increments (*see* 'Late retirement' above).

Living apart

You do not have to be living with your husband to claim a Category B pension. But as he must claim his pension before you can receive your own, you may have to check with the DSS periodically to find out when this has happened. The DSS says it will undertake this check, on request, every six months, and advises women in this position to make the first enquiry shortly before their husband reaches pensionable age.

Widows

The rules on widows will also change when the pension age for women is raised to 65. But in the meantime, if you were widowed before age 60 there are several options when you reach pension age. You can:

- claim your pension;
- continue to receive any widow's benefit to which you are already entitled until you do want to claim your pension (at 65 at the latest);

- defer receiving your pension and give up any widow's benefits you may be getting so that you qualify for increments on the pension when you claim it (at 65 at the latest).

Widows may be entitled to their own Category A pension (and the years during which widow's allowance or related benefits are paid will count towards qualifying years), a Category B pension under their late husband's NI contributions, or a composite Category A and B pension. A graduated pension may also be paid.

There are various ways of calculating the most favourable widow's pension and you should seek help from the DSS on this point. Widows may, in addition, be entitled to a pension under their husband's occupational scheme. If you were widowed after age 60, the calculations may be slightly different, but in effect the total pension, from whatever sources, is likely to be limited to the maximum single person's State pensions plus any increments.

Widowers face the same array of benefits as widows, with a few exceptions. The final pension will depend on your age when you became a widower and the age of your wife when she died. The DSS will help you to apply for the best combination of benefits.

The DSS will help you to apply for the best combination of benefits.

Divorced

Certain people whose marriages have ended in divorce or annulment may use the record of qualifying years of their former spouse instead of their own if their Category A basic pension is less than the full rate. Check with the DSS whether this applies in your case.

Key points

- If you want to find out what your State pension is worth, ask your local DSS office for a pension forecast (form BR19).
- To qualify for the full basic State pension you need a full NI contribution record for about 90 per cent of your working life.
- You may qualify for credits towards the pension if you qualify for Home Responsibilities Protection (HRP) or you receive certain other benefits.
- If your NI contribution record is insufficient you may be able to claim a pension based on your spouse's contribution record.
- You may still qualify for a State pension if you have worked abroad for several years.
- You cannot claim the State pension early, but you can defer the first payment and earn an increase in the rate.

16

Additional pension (SERPS) and how to claim your State pensions

- The current situation
- How the pension is calculated
- Contracting out of SERPS
- Graduated retirement benefit
- Pension forecast
- How to claim State pensions
- Appeals
- Pension pitfalls

Summary

The second tier of the State pension is the element that is linked to part of your earnings, known as 'additional pension' or SERPS (State Earnings-Related Pension Scheme). This pension, worth a maximum of about £120 per week, is paid at the same time as the basic pension – that is at age 65 for men and between age 60 and 65 for women, depending on when you retire.

The Government proposes to replace SERPS with the State Second Pension (SSP), converted from an earnings-linked pension to a flat-rate benefit. Eventually those earning over £9000 per annum will be encouraged, possibly forced, to opt out of the SSP and to start a private pension.

THE CURRENT SITUATION

If you are an employee and you are not 'contracted out' of SERPS, either through a company pension scheme or an 'appropriate' personal pension plan, automatically you will be a member of SERPS and pay for the pension through your National Insurance contributions. Unlike the basic State pension, where the minimum qualifying contribution period is about ten years to get any benefit at all, a right to SERPS builds up from day one. The value of the pension depends on the level of your earnings and the contribution period. It will also depend on when you reach pension age because the Government has reduced SERPS for those who retire after 5 April 1999. This, combined with the planned phased increase in women's pension age from 60 to 65, which kicks off in 2010, makes the calculation of the additional pension a mind-bogglingly complicated exercise.

HOW THE PENSION IS CALCULATED

Given the complexity of SERPS and the number of variables involved, the best way to check the value of your additional pension is through a pensions forecast, a free service from the Department of Social Security. For details, *see* page 197. If that's all you need, feel free to skip the next few pages.

Your SERPS pension will be based on your 'band earnings', that is earnings between the lower and upper threshold for National Insurance on which your contributions are based. The thresholds for 1999–2000 are £66 and £500 per week. The additional pension started with effect from the 1978–79 tax year. Broadly, the pension will be worth 25 per cent of band earnings averaged over the period from 1978–9 to 6 April 1999. For benefits built up after this date the formula is reduced over a ten-year period from 25 per cent to 20 per cent of band earnings averaged over your entire working life. (Try working this one out and you will realise why we don't complain about cuts to our State pensions until it is too late.)

Each April the State pensions are increased – usually in line with retail prices.

CONTRACTING OUT OF SERPS

You may belong to a company pension scheme that is contracted out of SERPS. In this case part of your and your employer's NI contributions are invested in the scheme, which effectively replaces SERPS with a private pension.

You can also contract out of SERPS if you have a special type of personal pension, although whether you should do so on an individual basis is another question. It is not easy to assess whether your contributions will build up a better pension within the State scheme or if they are invested in a private plan. Certainly those on lower earnings should stay in SERPS because the cost of running a personal pension will be disproportionately high for small contributions, particularly if sales commission is deducted. As for the rest, experts reckon that very broadly for the 1999–2000 tax year women are likely to be better off in SERPS but that men aged between 43 and 51 might benefit financially from contracting out.

Ironically, the Government's ambition to encourage people out of SERPS has not been helped by the massive computer problems it experienced in late 1998 and early 1999. Apart from delays in SERPS payments to pensioners, the rebates of NI contributions to those who have contracted out of SERPS were also delayed, resulting in the potential loss of returns on individual pension investments.

The rebate is calculated as a percentage of an employee's band earnings. For the 1998–9 tax year the NI thresholds were £64 (£3328 per annum) and £485 per week (£25 220 per annum), giving annual band earnings of £21 892. To give you an example of what the rebate might be worth, the rate for the 1998–9 tax year ranged from 3.4 per cent and 9 per cent of band earnings, depending on age. In monetary terms this meant that for those earning £25 220 or over, the rebate would range from about £740 at age 16 to about £1970 at age 46 and over.

The decision regarding SERPS should automatically be reviewed each year and whenever the Government reviews the contracting-out terms.

GRADUATED RETIREMENT BENEFIT

If you were employed between April 1961 and April 1975 and paid graduated NI contributions you will also qualify for a graduated retirement benefit. Don't get too excited – the level of benefit is very low. The maximum graduated pension for the 1999–2000 tax year is £6.20 per week for a woman and £7.40 for a man.

The amount you receive will depend on the number of 'units' of graduated contributions you paid during this period and the value of a unit at the time you claim your pension. The maximum number of units is 72 for a woman and 86 for a man. To find out the value of your entitlement, multiply the number of units by the unit value in force when you retire.

PENSION FORECAST

The pension forecast is a useful service provided by the DSS. If you want to find out what your State pension will be worth – and this is particularly important for those planning to retire early or who have short careers – the forecast provides a detailed breakdown of your entitlement. You can get a pension forecast provided you have more than four months to go to pensionable age.

You can get a pension forecast provided you have more than four months to go to pensionable age.

For a forecast of both your basic and additional State pensions, ask at your local DSS for form BR 19. If you just want to find out what your additional pension will be, ask for leaflet NP 38 and send the form it contains to the address shown. This type of forecast is intended to help you decide whether or not to contract out of the additional pension scheme, for example if you want to take out a personal pension plan.

Each forecast takes between three and six weeks to process, longer if you are widowed or divorced where the assessment will be more complicated. In due course the Government intends to ensure everyone receives an annual statement of their pension benefits to date.

HOW TO CLAIM STATE PENSIONS

Category A and B pensions

Most people are sent a claim form about four months before reaching State pension age. If you have not received one three months before that date then contact your local DSS. The Department of Social Security stresses: 'You should not rely on receiving a claim form direct from the DSS. We might not, for example, have your current address recorded or your date of birth might be different from the one we have.' Men receive two forms, so that if they are married their wives can also claim their Category B pension (if they are also over State pension age). (Where you want to claim an increased pension due to the death of your spouse, use the free death certificate issued by the Registrar when the death is reported.)

Together with the claim forms, the DSS also sends a letter providing details of the benefits for which you qualify. This will help you to decide whether to claim immediately or to postpone payment (*see* 'Late retirement', page 188). If you do not claim at State pension age, you will be reminded four months before age 70 for men and 65 for women (rising to 70 when equal pension ages are implemented). Bear in mind that you cannot earn any extra increments after these ages at present, although this is due to change.

Claims for extra pension for dependants must be made on a separate form.

Category D pensions for the over-80s

The Category D pension is paid to people who are 80 or older. If you already receive a pension when you reach 80 and the rate is less than that paid under Category D, the higher rate will normally be paid automatically.

Time limits for claims

You can claim your pension up to four months before and 12 months after the date from which you want to receive it. Do note the DSS warning:

> In no circumstances can your pension be back-dated more than 12 months before the date of your claim. You must claim an increase for a dependant not later than six months from the date on which you are entitled to it. In no circumstances can the increase be back-dated more than six months before the date of your claim.

When you choose the date from which you want to claim your pension, the DSS will set out the appropriate pay-days. The pension is paid from the first official pay-day following the date from which you claim. At the time of writing pay-day was Monday. The pension is paid direct into an account (for example a bank, building society, Girobank or post office account) or by a book of orders that you cash in at a post office of your choice (hence those awful queues in the post office on a Monday morning).

Whichever method you choose, do read carefully the notes that accompany your pension book, or are sent separately (in the case of payment to an account). The following section highlights the most important points.

APPEALS

Given the complexity of the State pension system it is not surprising that from time to time the DSS makes a mistake in the calculation of benefits. If you claim a social security benefit – whether it is your pension or some other form of payment – and you are unhappy about the decision made by the adjudication officer or adjudicating medical authority, you can request a review or make an appeal. However, first you should read leaflet NI 260 *A guide to reviews and appeals* to make sure you understand the rules.

You can request a review or make an appeal.

A review is a straightforward procedure (according to the DSS). It allows the adjudicating authorities to look at a case again and, if appropriate, change the decision quickly without the need for a full appeal. To give a rough idea of the grounds for review, you might have to prove one of the following:

- the decision on the pension was given in ignorance of an important fact;
- the decision was based on a mistake about an important fact;
- the decision was based on an error of law.

Before asking for a review you should request a full explanation of your assessment from your local DSS. If you are not satisfied, write to the office that gave the decision as soon as possible, since there is a time limit on payment of arrears where mistakes were made. The adjudication officer will settle your assessment or refer it to an appeals tribunal. The Social Security Appeal Tribunal (SSAT) hearing is your opportunity to state your disagreement with the adjudication officer's decision. The role of the tribunal is to establish the facts and then apply the relevant law to the case.

Who can appeal

The only person who can appeal is the claimant (the person claiming the benefit). However, you can appoint someone to speak on your behalf provided that person is approved by the DSS.

How to appeal

Write a letter or fill in the form in leaflet NI 246 *How to appeal*, available from the DSS or Jobcentres. You must provide details of the benefit claimed, your NI number or reference, the decision against which you are appealing, the date of the decision letter and why you think the decision is wrong. Sign and date your appeal and send it to the office that made the earlier decision. Write 'appeal' on the envelope and make sure you keep copies of all your documentation. Normally you only have three months from the date of the decision letter to submit an appeal.

Help is at hand

If the thought of making an official appeal is daunting, you can get independent advice on social security reviews and appeals from the Citizens Advice Bureau. Some people may qualify for Legal Aid, while others may be helped by their trade union.

Representation or witnesses

You can be represented at the hearing by anyone you feel can best put forward your case. It does not have to be someone with legal qualifications. Alternatively, you may feel you need some moral support, even if you plan to speak yourself. A witness or companion is welcome.

Even if you have a representative, statistics indicate that your chances of success will be improved if you attend as well. Of course if you are disabled or elderly this may not be possible. If you live abroad then you should get a friend or relative to represent you, possibly backed up by someone from the Citizens Advice Bureau.

Notification

Once the date for your hearing has been set, the tribunal clerk will send you copies of the documents associated with your case, and at the same time will tell you when and where to attend. You will be given at least ten days' notice.

PENSION PITFALLS

When you reach State pension age and start to draw the benefit, there are several important points to remember:

- Report any change in earnings (either your own or your spouse's) above the level set out in your pension notes, since this may affect your entitlement.
- An over-payment should not be regarded as a windfall – the DSS will track it down and, if the adjudication officer reckons you can repay, it will be deducted from future pension payments.

- Check your entitlement if you go into hospital or if you go into a home either temporarily or permanently. Your pension may be reduced where you receive in-patient treatment under the NHS either after six weeks or immediately if you were living in a local authority home before going into hospital.
- If you are going abroad, tell the DSS if it is likely to be for three months or more (you can only use the cash orders within three months of the date shown) and they will arrange for the money to be paid to you overseas. (If you plan to retire abroad, *see* Chapter 17);
- Report any changes to your personal and family circumstances, for example, marriage, divorce, death of a spouse or dependent relative.
- Do remember to include details of any pension payments in your income tax return.

Key points

- **If you are an employee you will automatically be in SERPS unless you contract out via a company scheme or an individual pension.**
- **The SERPS pension is worth up to a maximum of £120 at present.**
- **SERPS benefits, including the widow's pension, will be cut for anyone retiring after 6 April 2000.**
- **If you contract out of SERPS, your maximum rebate for the 1998–9 tax year will be between about £740 and £1970, depending on age.**
- **You should receive a form from the DSS regarding payment of your pensions about four months before reaching State retirement age (65 for men and between 60 and 65 for women, depending on when they were born).**
- **It is possible to appeal against the DSS assessment of your benefits.**

Further information

The Department of Social Security (DSS) publishes several guides to National Insurance and social security benefits which are available, free of charge, from local DSS offices. Some leaflets are also available from post offices and libraries:

Have your pension paid straight to your account

Attendance Allowance

Equality in State pension age: A summary of the Government's proposals

Retiring?

Benefits after retirement

Giving up your right to earn extra retirement pension

Retirement pensions and widows' benefits – Payment direct into a bank or building society account

Pensioners or widows going abroad

Over 80 pensions

There is a separate range of leaflets for former members of the armed forces and their dependants.

You can find out more about Legal Aid in England and Wales from the *Legal Aid Guide*, available from Legal Aid Head Office, Newspaper House, 8–16 Great New Street, London EC4 3BN. The equivalent service and guide for Scotland are available from: The Scottish Legal Aid Board, 44 Drumsheugh Gardens, Edinburgh EH3 7SW.

If you are living abroad and need legal advice with your appeal you may be eligible for free legal advice under the Legal Advice and Assistance Scheme. If you want to know the name and address of a solicitor who participates in the scheme in England or Wales, write to: The Law Society, 113 Chancery Lane, London WC2A 1PL. The address for Scotland is the same as the Scottish Legal Aid Board.

17

Working abroad

- Pension problems for expats
- State pensions and the expatriate
- Company pensions
- Offshore trusts
- Offshore plans
- Transfers

Summary

Foreign assignments are viewed by many employees as an exciting opportunity, while others regard the uprooting of family life to alien soil with, at best, grim acceptance. Whatever your attitude, evidence suggests that short- and long-term secondments overseas are on the increase as companies gear up for international business opportunities. Assignments can arise in virtually every corner of the globe, depending on the nature of the employer's business. But one of the most common locations for British company secondments is the European Union (EU). This is the main geographical area considered in this chapter, but most of the points apply also to other locations. Chapter 18 focuses on retiring abroad and how to take your pensions with you.

Do bear in mind that pensions are just one aspect of your pre-departure financial planning, whether working or retiring overseas. Well before you go you should seek expert tax advice to make the most of your UK personal allowances and exemptions on income tax and capital gains tax. A chartered accountant who specialises in expatriate tax law will also be able to advise you on your tax status – for example, there may be a good reason to apply for non-resident status as soon as possible.

PENSION PROBLEMS FOR EXPATS

The pay and benefits packages offered to expatriate employees vary considerably and must be carefully examined before acceptance. Levels of pay should compensate for the general disruption and for disparities between the cost of living in the UK and in the country of assignment. Help with rent, private medical insurance, disability insurance and even school fees are common features of the expatriate's package.

Surprisingly, pensions – although usually the most valuable benefit after pay – often are dealt with in a very piecemeal fashion by employers. The whole area of expatriate pensions is extremely complicated and it can be very difficult to quantify and compare the value of major benefits that do not have an obvious cash value. Unless you are confident that your company provides the best possible arrangement in terms of value and security, it is wise to seek expert advice.

One of the main problems for expatriates seconded within the EU (and virtually anywhere else, for that matter) is the absence of a workable cross border pensions regime. The tax structure of pension schemes is complicated enough on a national level, but when more than one regime is involved the system breaks down and the tax officials engage in a free-for-all.

Most European pension systems work on the basis of tax deferment. This means that there is tax relief on contributions and the build-up of the pension fund, but all or most of the pension itself is taxed in full as income. Quite understandably if Country A grants tax relief on contributions it will be keen to claim the tax on the pension itself, otherwise it will argue that the arrangement leads to a fiscal imbalance.

The European Commission has tried hard to create a pan-EU pensions structure for so-called 'mobile' or expatriate workers. To date its main achievement is to ease the situation for employees who work for the same employer and are sent abroad. In these cases the employee should be able to remain in the home country State and occupational schemes. In other words, if your company sends you to France or Italy, you will continue to build up your pension back in the UK if this is the best financial arrangement for your circumstances.

There are time limits on these quid pro quo arrangements but these vary depending on the employment circumstances. Certainly the system should work well for periods of up to five years, after which your employer may have to plead a special case to continue the arrangement.

Looking ahead, the number of workers whose career straddles several EU countries is increasing and the European Commission's long-term aim is to establish a legal and fiscal framework that provides for portable expatriate pension schemes for everyone, irrespective of whether they remain with the same employer or change jobs.

Know your rights

In the meantime it is essential to know your rights, to understand the impact of a foreign assignment on your pension, and to be sufficiently well informed to negotiate the best possible deal for yourself and your family. The following details cover the main aspects to consider when negotiating your expatriate pensions package. Do bear in mind though that these points offer general guidance only. Your contract should relate specifically to the actual assignment and must be tailored to cater for any particular problem areas.

Before considering what's on offer from your company it is wise to piece together a complete picture of the pension benefits you have built up to date and then to see how the secondment abroad will affect your State pension, occupational pension, company additional voluntary contributions (AVCs) and any private provision you may have made, for example through personal pensions.

It is essential to be sufficiently well informed to negotiate the best possible deal for yourself and your family.

STATE PENSIONS AND THE EXPATRIATE

State pensions are an important component in the overall picture and should not be overlooked by the expatriate. Chapters 14–16 explain how the State pension in the UK works and also explain how to get a 'pensions forecast' from the Department of Social Security (DSS) that tells you what your pension is likely to be worth.

The UK pension is rather meagre, to say the least, and will be further eroded over the coming decades. Elsewhere in Europe the State pension is worth much more and private company schemes are rare. In some countries – Spain and Greece, for example – the pension is worth over 90 per cent of national average earnings. Clearly then, if you work abroad for long periods and join the local social security scheme, it is important to keep track of any rights you build up to foreign State pensions, since these may provide a valuable source of income in retirement.

Assessing the value of overseas State pensions is not easy. Different countries apply different qualifying periods that set out the minimum number of years you must pay into the local national insurance system before a pension can be claimed (known as the 'vesting' period). In the UK it is normally necessary to work and pay full National Insurance contributions for at least ten years before you qualify for a proportion of the basic State pension, although benefits under the State Earnings-Related Pension Scheme (SERPS) build up from day one. In Belgium, however, an employee qualifies for a proportion of the State pension after just one year, whereas in Luxembourg, as in the UK, the minimum qualifying period is ten years. In Portugal and Spain the qualifying minimum is set even higher at 15 years. Without a pan-EU agreement it would be possible for an expatriate worker who moved around the EU to pay social security contributions for a full career and yet end up with little or no State pension simply because he or she had not completed the necessary qualifying period in each country of employment.

EU multilateral system

Fortunately, the EU has a very fair system in place, which is designed to ensure that expatriate employees do not lose out on their State pension rights as a result of single or multiple employment assignments within the member states.

As a general rule, when you work abroad for more than one year (technically, from day one) you must pay National Insurance or social security contributions in the country of assignment. There are a few exceptions to this, particularly where the assignment is expected to last for less than a year, or where the work covers several different countries, in which case it may be possible to stay in the UK scheme. Some social security agreements negotiated by the UK do allow for longer retention in the UK scheme but these arrangements tend to be made on an individual basis.

Assuming, however, that your assignments are for a longer period, then the Multilateral Agreement on Social Security allows you to combine the total number of years worked in the EU in order to meet minimum qualifying periods in each country. For example, if you work for 10 years in the UK, 8 years in Italy, 12 in Spain and 10 in Germany, the total number of years in which you paid NI or social security contributions is 40. This total more than satisfies every minimum qualifying period in the EU. Of course, you won't get a full pension from each country. The proportion of the pension will depend on the number of years you actually contributed.

Payment of the pension

To complicate matters further, State pension ages vary from country to country. Table 18.2 in Chapter 18 (page 223) provides the latest details at the time of writing, but bear in mind that several countries, including the UK, is raising the State pension age either just for women (to bring it in line with the male pension age) or for both sexes.

Payment of the pension, which is explained in more detail in Chapter 18, is usually dealt with by each country's social security department and paid in local currency. Each element of the pension is subject to the annual increases that apply in the country of source.

For the expatriate whose career spans several countries, it can be something of an administrative nightmare keeping track of all these foreign State pensions particularly where governments are in the process of changing the benefit structure to reduce costs. To avoid problems later, keep track of your social security number and the period you worked in each country. Supply these details to the relevant authorities at retirement.

Remember that exposure to different currencies will almost certainly lead to fluctuations in your overall income. In an ideal world any pensions earned under the EU Multilateral Agreement would be paid from a single source in a single currency, but at present this is no more than a proposal under consideration by the European Commission.

■ State pensions outside the EU

While the details above refer specifically to the EU, it is worth noting that the UK has social security agreements with many countries around the world, so, in theory at least, claiming your State pension should not present any serious problems. For details on payment of a UK pension overseas, *see* Chapter 18.

COMPANY PENSIONS

When it comes to company pensions there are several options to consider, including remaining in the UK scheme, joining the local scheme in the country of assignment and, as a last resort, setting up an offshore scheme or plan.

Whatever arrangement you settle for, it is important to check that you are not losing out in terms of the continuity and level of your pension benefits. For example, in some expatriate contracts employers guarantee that you will be no worse off as a result of your secondment than if you had stayed in the UK in the main company scheme.

■ Remaining in a UK scheme

The important point to note about private pension schemes in the UK – whether set up by an employer or by an individual – is that under normal circumstances you can only contribute if you have UK earnings. These 'relevant earnings' are defined very clearly by the Inland Revenue and as a rule do not include earnings paid by an employer while you are working abroad. Fortunately the UK tax authorities have for many years had one of the most flexible attitudes to employees who work abroad and generally it is possible to remain in the UK company scheme for up to ten years, provided your employer meets certain qualifying rules.

In November 1995 the Inland Revenue simplified the rules for employees who want to do just that. Previously you had to remain under the control of a UK employer while working overseas, but this is no longer necessary. For a trial period the Revenue has also dropped the requirement that you must have previously worked for the employer in the UK. This means new recruits can now work abroad from day one of their employment and still be able to join the UK pension scheme. The advantages of this arrangement are obvious, particularly if you plan to retire in the UK. All your benefits come from one source in one currency and you do not have to track down pension benefits from foreign employers when you come to retire in 20 years' time.

You should also consider the local company pension scheme.

Local schemes

If you are going abroad to work for a foreign employer you should also consider the local company pension scheme. Indeed you may have no choice if membership of the company scheme is a condition of employment (as it used to be in the UK until 1988). However, membership should entitle you to receive employer contributions and all the tax reliefs associated with locally approved pension arrangements. The downside is that you may have to work for several years to meet the minimum qualifying period for a pension and, even if you do, for legal reasons it may not be possible to transfer your benefits out of the country when you leave.

Potential tax problems

Taxation is the main stumbling block in any expatriate pension package – even if you remain in the UK scheme you may hit problems. Clearly, employees who claim relief on contributions in one country, but pay tax on the pension in another country, upset the fiscal balance. As a result, many foreign tax authorities will treat an expatriate's pension contributions paid by the UK employer to the UK scheme as extra income and will tax them accordingly. One way round the problem is to try to get compensation in your pay package for the extra tax levied. In practice, however, many companies maintain the pension promise but do not bother to fund it during the period the employee is abroad, particularly where this is for a short period. In other words, they guarantee the pension but do not set aside specific contributions to cover that guarantee. No employer contributions – no tax penalty in the country of assignment.

When the employee returns to the UK and rejoins the UK company's scheme, the Revenue usually will allow pension provision for all the years in service including the overseas secondment, provided the maximum pension is in line with what would have been earned if the employee had stayed in the UK. The notional UK salary can take account of promotions and inflation.

Clearly, then, it is not the pension promise that causes tax problems for the expatriate, but the funding of that promise – the payment of contributions on your behalf in order to build up the pension. If, to avoid these problems, your employer offers you an 'unfunded promise' where the usual pension benefits are provided for the period of secondment but there is no fund to back that guarantee, do seek legal advice and make sure the contract is watertight. For example, how safe would your pension be if the company went into liquidation or was taken over by a hostile predator? What would happen if you left to work for a rival company and tried to take a transfer of pension benefits? Where there is no specific fund earmarked for the pension covering the period of secondment this could prove very difficult.

OFFSHORE TRUSTS

Offshore pension trusts can be an effective and tax-efficient way of providing pension benefits for senior executives, particularly where the peripatetic nature of their career makes it impossible for them to remain within the UK company scheme. If you work for a UK company the trust would probably be held in the Channel Islands. Offshore pension trusts can be designed to provide higher benefits and earlier retirement than the main UK company scheme. Where you plan to retire abroad the trust can even be set up to pay your pension in a different currency.

However, do bear in mind that offshore trusts are complex and must be arranged by a reputable firm of employee benefits consultants and legal experts. Any arrangement should be backed by formal documentation and this should be checked by your own accountant or legal and tax adviser, provided they have expertise in this area. There can be all sorts of problems, for example hidden tax charges if you bring the fund back into the UK.

OFFSHORE PLANS

An increasing number of financial institutions sell long-term investment plans to expatriates from the Channel Islands, the Isle of Man, the Dublin international financial centre and other offshore locations. Some of these are designed to mirror pension plans in the UK, but they should not be confused with the real item because in most cases they cannot mirror the tax advantages of an onshore, Revenue-approved plan. However, some do offer limited tax advantages and it may be possible to transfer to a UK plan if you return home.

If you are interested in one of these plans, do watch out for high charges, which are endemic among offshore life office products. Also, check that the contract does not lock you in to a fixed period of contribution. If your secondment is cut short and you return to the UK you could face punitive early termination penalties. Be sure to consult an independent financial adviser who specialises in offshore products and in expatriate tax and pension planning. Make sure the adviser will also consider the wide range of offshore investment funds (similar to unit trust and unit-linked funds in the UK). These may provide better long-term growth prospects and prove more flexible than some of the insurance products.

Check that the contract does not lock you in to a fixed period of contribution.

TRANSFERS

If you leave your UK employer to work overseas you must also consider what to do with the pension benefits you have built up so far in the UK – whether in company schemes or private plans. Transfers represent one of the most complex areas of financial planning; if you face this problem read Chapter 10 which explains your main options when you leave a company scheme.

Transfers of pension benefits from a UK scheme to a foreign scheme are rare and in many cases may not be permitted by the overseas department of the Pension Schemes Office (part of the Inland Revenue). If you are planning to return to the UK after the overseas assignment it is almost certainly in your best interests to leave your pension where it is.

Key points

- **Check your State pension in the UK and ask the DSS how working abroad will affect your pension rights.**
- **Can you stay in your present company's scheme?**
- **Will the company guarantee that you will be no worse off than if you had remained in the UK?**
- **If the arrangement is unfunded (that is, not backed by employer and employee contributions), do check what would happen if, for example, the company becomes insolvent or you want to leave.**
- **If there is no company scheme then consider a local pension arrangement, provided your expected period of employment will allow you to meet the minimum qualifying periods.**
- **If you look for an offshore pension do beware the high charges associated with some of these plans and do not lock in to a long-term regular commitment.**
- **Don't forget to consider your tax status and to seek tax and investment advice from a qualified chartered accountant before going overseas.**

18

Retiring abroad

- Check your sources of pensions
- State pensions
- Company and private pensions
- Foreign pensions
- Dealing with the tax man

Summary

The prospect of retiring in the sun is very appealing. The choice of location may seem paramount, but if you want a financially healthy retirement it is important also to consider how all your pensions and other sources of income may be paid abroad without double tax penalties.

Up-to-date advice on pension and inheritance tax planning is essential before you leave the UK. This is a specialist subject, but there are several useful steps you can take in advance to reduce the administrative headache as well as your professional adviser's fees. It is equally important to seek tax and investment advice regarding your other assets.

CHECK YOUR SOURCES OF PENSIONS

Today's flexible career patterns tend to result in a bewildering variety of retirement benefits, but essentially there are three main sources of pension:

- State schemes;
- company schemes;
- private individual plans.

STATE PENSIONS

Chapters 14–16 deal with the UK State pensions in detail. Briefly, the pension, which builds up through payment of National Insurance contributions, is made up of two elements – a basic flat-rate benefit and an earnings-related supplement known as SERPS (State Earnings-Related Pension Scheme) or the 'additional' pension. The pension is paid at age 65 for men and between age 60 and 65 for women depending on when you retire. (The female State pension age is due to be raised in line with the male pension age and there is a transition period between 2010 and 2020 to achieve this.)

Cost-of-living increases

The Department of Social Security (DSS) confirmed that the State retirement pensions and widows' benefits can be claimed from anywhere in the world. However, annual cost-of-living increases are only paid if you live in the European Union or a country with which the UK has a social security agreement that provides for uprating (*see* Table 18.1).

This means that if you retire to Australia, Canada, New Zealand or any country not mentioned in the table your State pension will be frozen either at the time you leave the UK or, for those already abroad when they reach State retirement age, at the time of the first payment.

Table 18.1 Countries where your State pension qualifies for the annual increase

Austria	France	Malta
Barbados	Germany	Mauritius
Belgium	Gibraltar	Netherlands
Bermuda	Guernsey	Norway
Bosnia-Herzegovina	Iceland	Philippines
Cyprus	Irish Republic	Portugal
Denmark	Israel	Spain
Federal Republic of Yugoslavia	Italy	Sweden
Finland	Jamaica	Switzerland
Former Yugoslavia Republic of Macedonia	Jersey	Turkey
	Luxembourg	USA

Source: Department of Social Security, 1998

Clearly, the loss of the annual cost-of-living increases will rapidly erode the value of the pension over a 15–20-year retirement and extra income from other sources will be required to compensate. As a rough guide to the impact of inflation, £100 in your pocket today would be worth £64 in 15 years' time assuming 3 per cent annual inflation, and just £48 assuming an annual inflation rate of 5 per cent.

The only good news is that if you return to live in the UK, your State pension will be paid at the full current rate. UK expats on a temporary visit home can also claim the full rate but only for the period spent in the UK.

Short periods abroad

If you go abroad for short periods, the DSS makes special arrangements to pay your pension. No action is necessary where the period is less than six months. Pension payments must be claimed within three months of the due date, although you can get around this problem by having your pension paid into your UK bank or building society account, a National Savings account or to a person you nominate who lives in the UK.

If you plan to go abroad for longer than six months you must inform the DSS. Your pension can be paid as above or into an overseas bank. You can even ask the DSS to send the cheques to your overseas address. Alternatively, if you are overseas for two years or less, you can collect the lump sum on your return.

For over 12 months, a more permanent arrangement is made to pay your pension by automated credit transfer to your overseas bank.

COMPANY AND PRIVATE PENSIONS

Company and private individual pensions can also be paid abroad. If you want to check the value of your pension you should contact the pensions manager of the company scheme, or the financial institution – often an insurance company – in the case of a personal pension or similar contract.

Bear in mind that most statements that explain your future pension rights assume retirement is within the UK, so it is essential to check how retiring abroad will affect your tax position. For example, the tax-free cash lump sum that is an important feature of UK private pensions is not recognised in North America and if you receive the benefit there it may be taxed along with the pension. Also, remember that your pension will be subject to currency fluctuations. If the local currency in your retirement country rises against the pound, then the value of your UK pension will reduce in real terms. The only places where you are protected from this exchange risk are those which still use sterling, namely the Isle of Man and Gibraltar.

Most statements that explain your future pension rights assume retirement is within the UK.

Pensions from previous employment

Many people change jobs several times before reaching retirement, so it will be necessary to contact previous employers to check the value of any benefits you left in the former employers' schemes. These benefits are known as 'deferred' pensions. Where a company has been taken over or become insolvent and it is difficult to track down the trustees, the Pensions Register will trace your benefits free of charge (*see* details provided at the end of this chapter).

FOREIGN PENSIONS

If your career included overseas employment with foreign State and company pension entitlements the tracing problems could be multiplied tenfold. To add to the complications, foreign pensions may fall due at a different retirement age from the rest of your UK pensions (*see* Table 18.2).

As a general rule, whether you have State or company pensions, outside the UK it's up to you to keep track of your benefit rights and to make the claims. There is no central source of information about foreign State pensions, so you may have to contact each authority, although where there is a social security agreement with the UK the Department of Social Security will help.

DEALING WITH THE TAX MAN

Once you have checked your sources of pension it is time to examine how they will be taxed. Most of the tax details need to be sorted out at the time of retirement, but it is useful to know in advance how the system works and where the pitfalls lie. Expert advice is essential here and clearly the adviser must be conversant with the tax and pensions rules in the country of retirement. The object of the exercise is to pay tax on pensions and investment income just once – usually in your country of retirement.

Where the country you choose has a double taxation agreement with the UK (there are over 80 of these agreements in operation), the Inland Revenue will allow pensions to be paid gross. But first you will need a declaration from the foreign tax authorities stating that they are taxing you on your worldwide income. This declaration should be sent immediately to your UK tax office. If there is a delay your pensions will be taxed twice – once in the UK, at the basic rate of income tax, and once again in your country of retirement. However, if there is a delay in sending the form, the Inland Revenue confirms that the withholding tax can be reclaimed when it receives the declaration from the foreign tax authority.

Table 18.2 State pension ages in Europe

Country	*Men*	*Women*
Austria	65	60
Belgium[1]	65	61–65
Denmark	67	67
Finland	65	65
France[2]	60–65	60–65
Germany	65	65
Greece[3]	65	65
Ireland	65	65
Italy[4]	65	60
Luxembourg	65	65
Netherlands	65	65
Norway	67	67
Portugal	65	65
Spain	65	65
Sweden	65	65
Switzerland[5]	65	62
UK[6]	65	60–65

Notes: The ages shown assume you have completed the qualifying period of residence and/or contribution. In some countries earlier claims are possible.

1 The full pension builds up over 45 years for men and this will also apply to women in future. By 2009 the female state pension age will have risen in stages from 61 to 65.

2 The pension can be claimed at any time between 60 and 65, but the full benefit will only be paid after a full contributory career of 37.5–40 years.

3 For employees starting work after 1 January 1996 a common retirement age of 62 is applicable.

4 The female State pension age is 60 for those who started work before 31 December 1992.

5 The pension age is expected to equalise at 63 or 64 in due course.

6 The phased increase in the female retirement age to 65 will commence in 2010.

Source: Derived from statistics published by William M. Mercer, 1998

Tax havens not so heavenly

Finally, don't fall into the trap of thinking that if you move to a nil-tax environment you will escape with your pensions tax free. If you are lucky enough to retire to the Caymans or Bermuda, for example, you will find that there is no double tax treaty in force with the UK. If there is no local equivalent of the Inland Revenue, you will not be able to get the declaration that you are being taxed on your worldwide income. As a result the Revenue will impose the withholding tax on all your pensions paid from the UK.

Key points

- **Check the value of your State pensions (*see* 'Further information' below).**
- **Find out if your State pension will receive cost-of-living increases (*see* Table 18.1).**
- **Check the value of your UK company pensions, using the Pensions Register to trace any benefits from former employment if necessary.**
- **Check the expected value of any individual pension plans.**
- **Trace any overseas pension benefits (State and private).**
- **Find out how your pensions will be taxed in the retirement country.**

Further information

Ask at your local DSS for leaflet NI 106 *Pensioners or widows going abroad* and NI 38 *Social Security Abroad*. For further information on State pensions write to: Department of Social Security, Overseas Benefits Directorate, Payments Group, Longbenton, Newcastle upon Tyne NE98 1YX.

To get an idea of the value of your future State pension, ask your local DSS for the pension forecast form BR19. Also see page 219 on State pensions.

To trace pension benefits from former employment, contact: the Occupational Pensions Regulatory Authority, Invicta House, Trafalgar Place, Brighton, East Sussex BN1 4BY. Tel: 01273 627648.

19

What to do when things go wrong

- Common problems
- Guide to complaints
- Occupational pension schemes and OPAS
- Personal pensions
- Other sources of help

SUMMARY

Most company schemes and individual pension plans in the UK are well run, but from time to time things do go wrong. When the Mirror Group pension scheme members discovered £400 million had gone missing from their fund a national enquiry followed which led to the new Pensions Act (1995). A scandal of equally epic proportions was unearthed in the early 1990s by the Securities and Investments Board (the precursor to the Financial Services Authority), the chief financial services regulator, when it investigated the mass mis-selling of personal pensions to members of occupational schemes (*see* Chapter 10). Unfortunately, when fraud, theft, mis-selling or plain incompetence occur on a smaller scale the effect on individuals can be equally devastating but in the past help was not always so readily available.

The provisions of the new Pensions Act, most of which come into force in April 1997, require trustees to establish a two-stage internal dispute resolution process for members who have a complaint. This system will be the first port of call for any scheme member who has a problem or feels the scheme has in some way failed to provide the promised benefits. The Act also introduced a new regulator – the Occupational Pensions Regulatory Authority (OPRA), which supervises the security and complaints procedures. Trustees and the professionals who help run company pension schemes have a duty under the Act to report anything untoward to OPRA. It is too early to see how well these additional checks and balances work in practice, but any strengthening of dispute resolution and the regulation of schemes is welcome.

This chapter covers both occupational schemes and personal pensions. For contact details *see* Appendix 1.

COMMON PROBLEMS

So what problems are likely to arise? There are some very common battlegrounds for dispute in company schemes, many of which are investigated by the Occupational Pensions Advisory Service (OPAS – *see* page 229).

■ Transfers

The scandal over the mis-selling of personal pensions to members of occupational schemes is a massive problem for the regulators and is discussed in Chapter 10. However, this isn't the only transfer problem. Pension transfers are notoriously complicated. Employees often hit difficulties when they transfer from one employer's scheme to another. In the cases that OPAS investigates, the majority of enquiries stem from a total lack of understanding of how the transfer system works under a final salary scheme. This is hardly surprising, since only the scheme actuaries appear to know what is going on and even they have difficulty explaining the calculations.

■ Early retirement benefits

You may have problems if you negotiate early retirement, in particular if this is agreed as part of a redundancy programme or take-over/merger. The company's explanatory booklets may be ambiguous and there can be inconsistencies between the wording in the formal documentation and the requirements set by the employer. This problem is exacerbated by management promises – often made informally by unauthorised people – which the scheme trustees cannot deliver. (For pension considerations on early retirement, *see* Chapter 8.)

■ Benefits on winding up the scheme

Major legal and administrative obstacles prevent trustees from winding up (terminating) occupational pension schemes as quickly as they would like. As a result, scheme members may have to wait an unreasonably long time for the trustees to make clear what their benefit entitlements will be. The problem is particularly acute where scheme members actually pass pension age and should be drawing benefits. The recession triggered a sharp increase in the number of company failures and hence a corresponding increase in the number of complaints relating to pension scheme wind-ups.

Failure to provide statutory information

Scheme trustees have a legal duty to provide members with certain information about the scheme under what are known as 'disclosure' regulations. Failure to comply is mainly confined to smaller schemes and it has to be said that the complexity of the regulations does not help here. However, lack of disclosure of vital information cannot be excused and at times can conceal a much more serious underlying problem.

Misleading investment advice

OPAS and the Pensions Ombudsman sometimes get involved in cases where poor advice was given leading to the sale of an inappropriate product. The two most common examples relate to personal pensions sold to replace occupational scheme membership and, less frequently, plans sold to replace membership of the State Earnings-Related Pension Scheme.

Malpractice

The most common problem in this category is where contributions are deducted from employees' pay but somehow never quite make it into the pension scheme fund. This invariably occurs where the employer is in financial difficulties and is desperately searching for any means possible to increase cash flow. OPAS has also seen several cases where cheques issued by insurers to pay scheme benefits have found their way into overdrawn company bank accounts and are effectively 'lost' when the company then goes into liquidation. The only way round this is for insurers to issue benefit cheques direct to scheme members.

GUIDE TO COMPLAINTS

The UK financial services sector has various agencies that deal with complaints and queries. This section explains how to get help and the procedures to follow if your problem relates to an occupational scheme or individual pension plan. For queries about your State pension, *see* Chapter 16.

If your pension complaint relates to a personal plan the Personal Investment Authority Ombudsman may get involved, particularly where you complain about the advice you were given at the time of the sale. Most complaints about occupational schemes go to OPAS, but where the service fails to resolve the complaint it passes it on (with your permission) to the Pensions Ombudsman who has statutory power to enforce rulings.

Most complaints about occupational schemes go to OPAS.

Of course you may have bought your pension plan or small company scheme through a firm of stockbrokers, solicitors or accountants. In this case you will deal in the first instance with the appropriate self-regulatory organisation or recognised professional body. The procedure is described briefly later in this chapter.

OCCUPATIONAL PENSION SCHEMES AND OPAS

OPAS is a grant-aided, non-profit-making company limited by guarantee. It is an independent and voluntary organisation providing free help and advice to members of the public. The OPAS service is available to anyone who believes they have pension rights. This includes:

- the 'active' scheme member – the employee still at work;
- pensioners;
- those with 'deferred' pensions from previous employment;
- all the dependants of the above, for example, spouses, children and possibly common law partners.

Step 1: Contact the scheme authorities

The first step is to contact the scheme authorities. Only after you have attempted to resolve your problem this way will OPAS step in. Under a company scheme the scheme authorities will be the trustees, although they may have delegated this responsibility to the personnel or pensions department. If so, they will tell you who to contact and where. If you don't know who the trustees of your scheme are, look in your scheme booklet, where it should be clearly stated.

Under the Pensions Act the trustees must put in place a formal disputes system. This will be in two stages. Stage one simply allows you to make your complaint and be guaranteed a hearing. You should receive a decision from the trustees within two months. If you are not satisfied, you then have the right to ask for your case to be reconsidered. You will have six months to make up your mind whether to pursue your complaint further, and again the trustees have two months to reply.

With a personal pension the scheme authorities are the plan providers. This will be a life assurance company, unit trust group, investment trust group, building society or bank. If you bought your plan through an independent adviser, this firm will be your first port of call.

Step 2: Put it in writing

Once you have identified the correct authorities, put your complaint in writing. There is no formal time-scale for personal pension disputes, but two months is considered a reasonable time under the Pensions Act for company scheme trustees to reply, so this would seem a sensible deadline for a response in the case of personal pension complaints. Keep a copy of the letter and all original documents. If you do not receive a reply within the stated time, or you are dissatisfied with the response, then you can ask OPAS for help.

Step 3: Contact OPAS

The best way to approach OPAS is through your local Citizens Advice Bureau (CAB) which will put you in touch with your nearest OPAS adviser. If there is no CAB locally then send a brief letter direct to OPAS, enclosing any relevant material, for example:

- policy documents (personal pensions only);
- the trust deed and rules;
- the scheme booklet;
- a covering letter giving OPAS permission to approach the scheme authorities on your behalf.

The OPAS adviser may require other documents in due course, so you should make sure your file is up to date with any pension scheme announcements and annual benefit statements.

How OPAS can help

There are four ways in which OPAS can help you sort out your problem.

- Pension schemes are extremely complicated and scheme authorities often fail to communicate with members in plain English. OPAS advisers can translate the jargon and set your mind at rest by confirming that you are being treated fairly, where this is the case.
- When you have a legitimate complaint, OPAS can approach the scheme authorities on your behalf, or help you to make a further approach yourself.
- You may have a general enquiry on a pensions matter. If you are directly affected, OPAS can provide an answer you will understand.
- OPAS will explain how and when other complaints authorities can help. The two most closely related organisations are the Pensions Ombudsman and the Personal Investments Authority Ombudsman. If you are not sure which office you should approach first, contact OPAS.

What OPAS cannot do

OPAS operates by negotiation and conciliation. It does not have statutory powers to enforce its decisions and relies on the pension company, employer or adviser to co-operate, either because they have made a genuine mistake or because they do not want the unwelcome publicity the case might attract (*see* below, 'Enter the Pensions Ombudsman'). OPAS does not assist members of the public who have a grievance, except where they have a legitimate cause for complaint. In other words, if you think your scheme offers a very low level of pension or death-in-services benefits, provided the trustees are acting in accordance with the scheme rules there is nothing OPAS can do. Finally, OPAS cannot give personal financial advice, for example in the selection of a pension provider. If you need this type of help, *see* Chapter 1.

Enter the Pensions Ombudsman

If OPAS fails to rectify the problem, then you can turn to the Pensions Ombudsman. While OPAS has an outstanding track record on settling disputes, nevertheless there will always be the stubborn cases where the scheme authorities refuse to budge even if it is clear that they are in the wrong. On other occasions OPAS might uncover a serious case concerning fraud or some other illegal activity in which case arbitration and conciliation are not the appropriate methods to tackle the problem. These cases are referred by OPAS to the Pensions Ombudsman (whose office, incidentally, is just down the corridor from OPAS) or, if appropriate, to the Financial Services Authority Ombudsman or one of the other regulatory authorities established to oversee the financial services sector.

The Pensions Ombudsman is completely independent and acts as an impartial adjudicator.

The Pensions Ombudsman was appointed under the Social Security Act 1990 to deal with complaints against and disputes with occupational schemes and personal pensions. The Pensions Ombudsman is completely independent and acts as an impartial adjudicator. Services of the Pensions Ombudsman are free and decisions made by the Ombudsman are enforced by statutory power. The current

Ombudsman has a reputation and proven track record for taking tough, decisive action. However, the Ombudsman stresses that cases should always go to OPAS first. If the Ombudsman investigates and decides there is no justified complaint, you cannot then go to OPAS. If you go to OPAS first and OPAS then refers the case to the Ombudsman you effectively get two bites of the cherry.

What happens next?

Assuming you have been to OPAS and the service feels your complaint is suitable, it will pass on to the Ombudsman all the documentation it holds. In addition you should write directly to the Ombudsman outlining the problem, quoting the OPAS reference number. Provided the problem falls within the remit of the Pensions Ombudsman, your case will be investigated and a decision made. This will include a decision on any compensation, if appropriate. You will receive a written statement from the Ombudsman, as will the pension scheme or employer. This decision is final and binding on both you and the pension scheme/employer – subject only to an appeal to the High Court or Court of Session on a point of law.

All complaints and disputes are treated in confidence. If the Ombudsman needs to disclose details to anyone other than the relevant scheme or employer your permission will be asked first.

PERSONAL PENSIONS

Personal pensions complaints cover a wide area and fall under the remit of both the Financial Services Authority (FSA) and the Pensions Ombudsman. If in doubt write to OPAS or the FSA, both of which act as an unofficial sorting office for pensions complaints and will make sure your details go to the right place. Briefly, under the Financial Services Act, if a company sold you an inappropriate product for your needs you may be able to claim compensation.

If you have a personal pension complaint, write to the compliance officer at the company which sold you the product. You should receive an acknowledgment of your letter within seven days, but allow two months for the actual investigation before taking the case to the ombudsman or regulator. The company's letterhead should show the details of the regulator but if not, contact the Financial Services Authority central register (*see* 'Further information' on page 236).

OTHER SOURCES OF HELP

Trade unions

Trade unions can be a valuable source of information and help with company pensions queries and complaints. Some unions – the GMB for example – have a dedicated pensions department run by experts. Others will have at least one expert on pensions and might also use the services of an outside adviser.

Trade unions may provide financial support for court cases where they believe the scheme member had been treated unfairly, although in the first instance they are likely to help you take your case to OPAS and the Pensions Ombudsman.

Pensions Registry

The Pensions Registry and Tracing Service was launched in 1990 to help individuals trace their pension benefits if they have lost touch with a former employer. This often happens when a company changes its name and address, is taken over or becomes insolvent. The service is now part of the Occupational Pensions Regulatory Authority (OPRA – *see* page 243). All schemes, with a few minor exceptions, are required to register with the service and to provide the following details:

- scheme name and address (and previous names since 6 April 1975);
- scheme status (for example, open to new members, closed to new members, 'paid up' – that is, no longer taking new contributions);
- number of active members;

- Inland Revenue reference number of scheme;
- name and address of insurance company (if any) involved;
- names of trustees and administrator of the scheme;
- names and addresses of all employers connected with the scheme since 6 April 1975.

Officially the scheme only covers pension scheme details from April 1975, but since some schemes provide information for earlier years it is always worth asking if the service can trace a pension dated pre-1975.

Most requests for information on lost pensions are sorted out within two days and the scheme reports a success rate of almost 90 per cent. Where delays occur this is usually because the applicant has insufficient information. The tracing request form asks for the name of the employer, the trading name (if different), the address, any previous trading names and addresses, the name of the scheme and the address of the management of the scheme. If any of these details are missing it might take the registry some time to trace the pension, particularly if the former employer has gone out of business altogether.

Key points

- Write to trustees or scheme authorities (keep original copies of important documents).
- In the case of an individual plan write to the firm that gave you the advice and if necessary to the relevant regulator.
- If dissatisfied, contact OPAS via the Citizens Advice Bureau.
- Check you have all the relevant documents for a first interview.
- Be prepared to accept a satisfactory explanation – your complaint may prove unfounded.
- Be prepared to go to the Pensions Ombudsman if OPAS cannot resolve the case.

Further information

Contact the Financial Services Authority at Gavrelle House, 2–4 Bunhill Row, London EC1Y 8RA. Consumer helpline: 0845 6061234.

Appendix 1

Financial planning and investment advisers

Where no telephone number is provided, the organisations below prefer you to contact them by post. Before you appoint a firm to act on your behalf, you can check with the chief regulator, the Financial Services Authority (FSA) that it is authorised and registered with the appropriate regulator. To contact the **FSA central register**, telephone 0171 929 3652.

Stockbrokers and investment managers

Association of Private Client Investment Managers and Stockbrokers (APCIMS)

112 Middlesex Street, London E1 7HY

Tel: 0171 247 7080; e-mail info@apcims.co.uk; website www.apcims.co.uk

Publishes a free directory of member firms, many of which provide a full financial planning service.

Financial planners and advisers

Institute of Financial Planning (IFP)

Whitefriars Centre, Lewins Mead, Bristol BS1 2NT

The IFP is multi-disciplinary and its members are well qualified in giving independent planning advice. For the register of Fellows of the Institute, telephone 0117 930 4434.

Society of Financial Advisers (SOFA)

20 Aldermanbury, London EC2V 7HY

Tel: 0171 417 4419

Part of the Chartered Insurance Institute and a major examiner of independent advisers and life assurance company sales staff.

Independent advisers

For a list of three local independent advisers, contact **IFA Promotion** on 0117 971 1177. For fee-based independent advisers contact the **Money Management Register** on 0117 976 9444.

Accountants

Institute of Chartered Accountants in England and Wales

Moorgate Place, London EC2P 2BJ

Tel: 0171 920 8100/8711

About 700 members of the Institute of Chartered Accountants are qualified to offer a full advisory service, but members of other taxation bodies can also help.

Institute of Chartered Accountants in Scotland

27 Queen Street, Edinburgh EH2 1LA

Tel: 0131 225 5673

Association of Chartered Certified Accountants (ACCA)

29 Lincoln's Inn Fields, London WC2A 3EE

Tel: 0171 242 6855

Chartered Institute of Taxation and Association of Tax Technicians

12 Upper Belgrave Street, London SW1X 8BB

Tel: 0171 235 9381

Chartered tax advisers and members of this institute specialise purely in tax work for companies and for individuals.

Solicitors

The Law Society of England and Wales

113 Chancery Lane, London WC2A 1PL

Tel: 0171 242 1222

The Law Society of Scotland

26 Drumsheugh Gardens, Edinburgh EH3 7YR

Tel: 0131 226 7411

The Law Society of Northern Ireland

Law Society House, 98 Victoria Street, Belfast BT1 3JZ

Tel: 01232 231614

Solicitors are strongly represented in the financial services market. Two organisations dedicated to professional independent advice are:

Solicitors for Independent Financial Advice (SIFA)

Telephone helpline 01372 721172

Association of Solicitor Investment Managers (ASIM)

Chiddingstone Causeway, Tonbridge, Kent TN11 8JX

Tel: 01892 870065

Pension specialists

Association of Consulting Actuaries (ACA)

No 1 Wardrobe Place, London EC4V 5AH

Tel: 0171 248 3163

Fax: 0171 236 1899

Membership of ACA includes most firms of consulting actuaries and individuals engaged in private practice. Only qualified actuaries with a minimum of three years' experience are entitled to become full members of the ACA.

Association of Pension Lawyers (APL)

c/o Paul Stannard, Travers Smith Braithwaite, 10 Snow Hill, London EC1A 2AL

Tel: 0171 248 9133

Fax: 0171 236 3728

The APL membership includes solicitors and other firms with a special interest in legal aspects associated with pension schemes.

Association of Pensioneer Trustees

c/o Fairmount Trustee Services Ltd, Fairmount House, Bull Hill, Leatherhead, Surrey KT22 7AY

APT represents the interests of those who act as 'pensioneer trustees' for small self-administered schemes.

Faculty of Actuaries in Scotland

23 St Andrew Square, Edinburgh EH2 1AQ

Tel: 0131 557 1575

Fax: 0131 557 6702

Works closely with the Institute of Actuaries in London and is one of the two UK bodies that control the professional qualifications of actuaries. The Faculty and Institute also act as 'recognised professional bodies' (RPBs) and regulate their members under the Financial Services Act.

Institute of Actuaries

Staple Inn Hall, High Holborn, London WC1V 7QJ

Tel: 0171 242 0106

Fax: 0171 405 2482

For details *see* Faculty of Actuaries in Scotland above.

National Association of Pension Funds (NAPF)

12–18 Grosvenor Gardens, London SW1W 0DH

Tel: 0171 730 0585

Fax: 0171 730 2595

Has 1200 fund members, including most of the largest employers in the private and public sectors, and over 300 other members providing professional services to pension funds. The Association provides information, training and runs regular conferences.

Occupational Pensions Advisory Service (OPAS)

11 Belgrave Road, London SW1V 1RB

Tel: 0171 233 8080

Fax: 0171 233 8016

Provides a free service to pension scheme members, pensioners, deferred pensioners and their dependants who have a problem or complaint about their scheme.

(*See* Chapter 19 for how to use the service.)

Occupational Pensions Regulatory Authority (OPRA)

Invicta House, Trafalgar Place, Brighton, East Sussex BN1 4DW

Tel: 01273 627648

Fax: 01273 627630

The statutory regulator for company pension schemes in the UK.

Pensions Management Institute (PMI)

PMI House, 4–10 Artillery Lane, London E1 7LS

Tel: 0171 247 1452

Fax: 0171 375 0603

The professional institute for those working in the pensions industry. It provides tuition and sets examinations leading to nationally recognised qualifications.

Pensions Ombudsman

11 Belgrave Road, London SW1V 1RB

Tel: 0171 834 9144

Fax: 0171 821 0065

Complaints or disputes that cannot be resolved by OPAS (*see* above) may be investigated by the Pensions Ombudsman who has statutory power to enforce decisions. (*See* Chapter 19 for how to use the service.)

Pre-Retirement Association (PRA)

Nodus Centre, University Campus, Guildford, Surrey GU2 5RX

Tel: 01483 39350

National association for pre-retirement education in the UK, providing training for counsellors and co-ordinating courses around the country.

Registrar of Pension Schemes

Occupational Pensions Board, PO Box 1NN, Newcastle upon Tyne NE99 1NN

Tel: 0191 225 6394

Fax: 0191 225 6390

Operates a free tracing service for pension scheme members who have lost touch with a former employer's scheme. All schemes must register by law.

Society of Pension Consultants (SPC)

Ludgate House, Ludgate Circus, London EC4A 2AB

Tel: 0171 353 1688

Fax: 0171 353 9296

A representative body for firms and individuals working as pensions and employee benefits consultants.

Other useful organisations

Association of British Insurers (ABI)

51 Gresham Street, London EC2V 7HQ

Tel: 0171 600 3333

Fax: 0171 696 8999

A trade association for insurance companies and provides useful statistics and other information on individual and company pensions.

Association of Investment Trust Companies (AITC)

Durrant House, 8–13 Chiswell Street, London EC1Y 4YY

Tel: 0171 431 5222

The trade body for investment trusts. Its directory, *The Complete Guide to Investment Trusts*, price £16.94, is available from PBI Publishing, Tel: 0171 638 1916.

The Association of Unit Trusts and Investment Companies (AUTIF)

65 Kingsway, London WC2B 6TD

Tel: 0171 831 0898

The trade body for unit trusts and open-ended investment companies. It publishes a range of free fact sheets which explain how these investments work.

The Stock Exchange

London EC2N 1HP

Tel: 0171 797 1000

Publishes useful leaflets on buying and selling shares and on rolling settlement and nominee accounts.

Public/government agencies

Department of Social Security (DSS)

The Adelphi, 1–11 John Adam Street, London WC2N 6HT

Tel: 0171 962 8000

Government Actuary's Department (GAD)

22 Kingsway, London WC2B 6LE

Tel: 0171 242 6828

Fax: 0171 831 6653

Inland Revenue (Savings and Investment Division)

South West Wing, Bush House, London WC2B 4RD

Tel: 0171 438 6622

Occupational Pensions Regulatory Authority (OPRA)

Invicta House, Trafalgar Place, Brighton, East Sussex BN1 4BY

Tel: 01273 627648

Fax: 01273 627630

OPRA took over from OPB in April 1997.

Pension Schemes Office (PSO)

Lynwood Road, Thames Ditton, Surrey KT7 0DP

Tel: 0181 398 4242

Fax: 0181 398 7333

also at:

St Nicholas Court, Castle Gate, Nottingham NG1 7AR

Tel: 01602 243855

Fax: 01602 504355

Appendix 2

Glossary of terms

Pensions people like jargon, a passion fuelled by Government departments' and regulators' eagerness to fell rainforests and add to the complexity of the rules. As a result, there is little hope that consumers will ever really understand what is going on. If they did, the need for interpreters would disappear, along with half the pension providers and schemes that offer bad value for money. Until that day, the following guide to pensions jargon may help. For details about specific organisations *see* Appendix 1.

Accrual rate

The rate at which the scheme member's pension rights build up. In a 'sixtieths' scheme your pension would build up at a rate of one-sixtieth of your final salary for each year of service. In this case it would take 40 years to build up the maximum pension allowed by the Inland Revenue of forty-sixtieths, or two-thirds of final salary (subject to restrictions in the case of some higher earners – *see* **earnings cap**).

Accrued benefits

The benefits and rights you have built to date. Also known as 'accrued rights'.

Active investment management

Active managers use in-house and external research, together with their own detailed knowledge of companies and their management teams, in order actively to select the stocks. Both **balanced** and **specialist managers** work in this way. *See also* **passive investment management**.

Actuarial valuation

An investigation by an actuary to assess how well a pension fund is able to meet its liabilities in terms of pensions, lump-sum death-in-service payments and other benefits. The actuary is then able to recommend any necessary changes to the contributions paid by the employer or to any **discretionary benefits** paid to members.

Actuary

Actuaries are the number crunchers and the risk assessors. The actuary's job is to look at what benefits the fund must pay out in 20 or 30 years' time and calculate how much needs to be paid in now to meet those liabilities. To do this they will take into account mortality statistics (for example, to estimate how many people are likely to draw pension to 100 and how many are likely to die young) and potential investment returns. Consulting actuaries are hired by employers and trustees to provide a range of services, including pension scheme design, advising on the appointment of the **investment manager**, performance measurement, scheme administration and trustee training.

Added years

Where the pension is expressed as a proportion of final salary – typically it will build up at the rate of one-sixtieth of final salary for each year of service. Some **additional voluntary contribution** (AVC) schemes allow members to top up their main pension scheme benefits by investing to build up extra 'years'.

Additional voluntary contributions (AVCs)

Extra contributions to a separate fund paid by the member in addition to the main scheme contributions. Total employee contributions to the main scheme and AVC combined must not exceed 15 per cent of annual earnings. AVCs are normally run by insurance companies and building societies although an increasing number of unit trust groups are entering this market. *See also* **free-standing additional voluntary contributions**.

Allocation rates

One of two methods used by life offices to deduct extra charges from your premiums in order to pay commission to the adviser or representative. Here the provider allocates a small percentage of your premiums to units – in other words a hefty chunk is deducted before investment, often about 30 per cent. On a long-term plan the period of low allocation is usually about two years and will be repeated for any increments to your premiums. *See also* **capital levy**.

Annuity

Provides a guaranteed income, usually for life, in return for a lump-sum investment. 'Compulsory purchase annuities' (CPAs) must be bought with the bulk of the proceeds from a **money purchase pension** while 'purchased life annuities' (PLAs) are bought voluntarily with spare capital. The main difference is that the income from CPAs is taxed in full, while only the interest element of the income from a PLA is taxed; the element that represents a return of capital is not taxed.

Appointed representative

Companies that have a contract with a life office to sell one or more of its products on an exclusive basis in return for a commission payment. The appointed representative is not necessarily part of the life company and may sell other financial products on an independent basis.

Appropriate personal pension

Introduced in 1988, the appropriate personal pension allows employees who are not members of a 'contracted-out' company pension scheme to contract out of the **State Earnings-Related Pension Scheme** (SERPS) on an individual basis in return for a rebate of **National Insurance** contributions which are invested in your chosen plan. The rebate is related to age.

Asset classes

The main sectors in which pension funds invest, including UK **equities**, overseas **equities**, UK **bonds** (fixed-interest), index-linked **gilts**, **cash** and **property**.

Asset/liability modelling

Matching what the pension fund owns and how it is invested with the guaranteed benefits it must pay in terms of pensions and lump sums to members who retire, leave the company or die.

Balanced manager/fund

A balanced manager determines the allocation of assets between the main investment sectors (for example, cash, equities, property, bonds) and also selects the individual securities within each sector. *See also* **specialist manager**.

Band earnings

National Insurance for employees is levied on what are known as 'band earnings', that is earnings between lower and upper limits (known as the **lower earnings limit** or LEL, and the **upper earnings limit** or UEL). These are £66 and £500 per week (£3432 and £26000 per annum) for the 1999–2000 tax year.

Basic State pension

A flat-rate benefit (also known as the 'old-age pension') that is paid to individuals who reach State pension age and have paid or been credited with sufficient **National Insurance** contributions during their **working life**. Women can also claim for a smaller dependant's pension through their spouse's NI contributions.

Beneficiaries

In the case of a pension fund the beneficiaries – those who benefit from the trust – are current members, deferred members (ex-employees who have left behind their pension rights), retired employees drawing pensions and all the dependants of these people.

Bid/offer spread

The difference between the offer price – the price at which you buy units – and the bid price – the price at which you can sell units – creates an initial charge, usually of 5 per cent. This dual pricing system serves little purpose other than to confuse. The important point to remember is that the real value of your units is the bid price because that is what you will get if you want to cash in your investment.

Bonds

UK bonds are issued by borrowers who undertake to repay the principal sum on a specified date, rather like an IOU. During the time that the bond is outstanding, a fixed rate of interest is paid. *See also* **gilts**.

Buyout bond

Used to take a transfer of pension benefits. Sold by life offices and similar to a personal pension, although the buyout bond retains the valuable **guaranteed minimum pension**, unlike the personal pension which offers the non-guaranteed **protected rights**. However, unlike a **personal pension**, it is not possible to pay extra contributions to a buyout bond.

Capital levy

One of two methods used by life offices to deduct extra charges to pay commission to the adviser or representative who sells the product. 'Capital units', which are purchased during the 'initial' period, bear a much higher annual management charge than ordinary or 'accumulation' units. The charge usually continues throughout the entire period of the contract. Initial commission is also paid on any increments you make to the level of premium. *See also* **allocation rates**.

Carry back/carry forward

A special provision that exists for employees and the self-employed who have unused tax relief in previous years and want to make a substantial personal pension payment. Through the Inland Revenue's carry back and carry forward rules it is possible to 'mop up' unused tax relief for up to seven previous tax years by treating a payment this year as though it had been made in a previous tax year.

Cash
In the context of pension funds, 'cash' investments are similar to a building society or bank deposit account.

Commission/commission reinvestment
Remuneration paid by the life office to the adviser or representative on the sale of a product. The level of commission depends on the type of product, the amount invested and the term of the contract. The commission can be reinvested into the plan if the adviser works on a fee basis. This is known as nil commission or non commission terms.

Commutation
See **tax-free cash**.

Company representative
Also known as direct salesmen and tied agents. Company representatives are employed directly by the life office and work solely for that company.

Compulsory purchase annuity (CPA)
See **annuity**.

Consulting actuary
See **actuary**.

Contracted out/contracted in
Most company pension schemes in the UK are 'contracted out' of the **State Earnings-Related Pension Scheme** (SERPS) and pay a reduced rate of employee and employer National Insurance contribution. The difference between the full and reduced-rate contribution is invested to provide a level of pension that broadly matches what members would have got under SERPS. (Some older schemes guaranteed to match the SERPS benefits through guaranteed minimum pensions.) Some schemes are based on **final salary**, others on **money purchase** – for example, the contracted-out money purchase scheme (COMP). There is also a contracted-in money purchase scheme (CIMP).

Contribution
Regular payments or premiums made to pension schemes and plans.

Contribution holiday
Where the employer (and, rarely, the employee as well) stops paying pension contributions for a period of time, usually because the scheme actuary has identified a **surplus** of assets over liabilities in the fund. Effectively this means that the fund is bigger than necessary to pay the guaranteed pension and lump-sum benefits. Rather than increase benefits,

most employers attempt to treat a surplus as a lucky windfall, although sometimes the courts put a stop to this game.

Contribution limits

The Inland Revenue sets out maximum contributions that an individual can pay each year. In a company scheme employees can pay up to 15 per cent of **pensionable pay** while in a **personal pension** the limit is between 17.5 and 40 per cent of **net relevant earning**, depending on age. The employer's contributions are not restricted under a company scheme, but are included under the personal pension limits.

Death-in-retirement benefits

The pension and lump sum paid to the deceased member's spouse and/or other dependants where death occurs in retirement.

Death-in-service benefits

The pension and lump sum paid to the deceased member's spouse and/or other dependents where death occurs while still employed.

Deferred pensioner

A scheme member who changes employment and leaves behind his or her pension benefits. The benefits are known as a deferred pension because the pension is held by the scheme until retirement age.

Deficit

In pension fund terms a deficit is identified when the fund cannot meet its liabilities in terms of the guaranteed benefits it must pay. *See also* **surplus**.

Defined benefit

A term for final salary schemes. These are pension schemes that link your pension to your salary – usually at or just before retirement. Usually there is no direct link between what you pay in and the emerging pension.

Defined contribution

Money purchase pensions, where there is no direct link between the pension and your salary at retirement.

Dependants

In the context of a pension scheme, the members' or beneficiaries' dependants are usually limited to the spouse and children under 18. However, some schemes allow common law partners to be classed as beneficiaries. 'Members' has a wider context than working employees who are members of the scheme. It also refers to pensioners and those with deferred pensions – that is employees who have changed jobs but have left behind their scheme benefits.

Deposit account pensions

A choice of pension fund that is run in a similar way to a building society account except there is tax relief on the contributions and tax-free roll-up of the fund.

Derivatives

Complex creatures that should be treated with caution. 'Futures' involve agreeing to buy or sell assets in the future at a price set today. You might also take out an 'option' to buy or sell at a pre-agreed price but not exercise that right. Investment managers use derivatives mainly to reduce risk. Derivatives are used in retail pension funds to guarantee a proportion of stock market growth and to protect the price of your investment falling below a predetermined limit.

Disclosure regulations

Pension scheme trustees are required by law to send to members and in some cases to make available on request certain information about the scheme and the benefits.

Discretionary benefits

Non-guaranteed benefits, although in some cases they can become an expectation – typically where pension increases above the guaranteed minimum are paid on a regular basis. Discretionary payments are paid at the 'discretion' of the **trustees**. The trust deed and rules, for example, may include a 'discretion' to allow trustees to pay death benefits and spouse's pensions to common law partners.

Discretionary management

A discretionary investment service is where the investment manager has virtually total control over which sectors and stocks are selected, apart from any pre-agreed restrictions set by the **trustees**.

Dividend

See **equities**.

Earnings cap

Introduced in the 1989 Budget, the cap restricts the amount of salary on which pension contributions and benefits are based. For the 1999–2000 tax year the earnings cap is £90 600. The cap applies to members of final salary schemes set up after the 1989 budget and members who joined any final salary scheme on or after 1 June 1989. It also affects everyone with a **personal pension**.

Equities

UK equities are the quoted shares of companies in the UK and account for up to 60 per cent of most pension funds. Companies 'go public' by being quoted on the Stock Exchange or Unlisted Securities Market in order to raise finance by issuing shares. A 'share' literally entitles the owner to a specified share in the profits of the company and, if the company is wound up, to a specified share of its assets. Owners of shares are entitled to the dividend – the annual or six-monthly distribution to shareholders of part of the company's profits. Overseas equities are similar but confer different shareholders' rights.

Executive pension plan (EPP)

A special fast-track plan for executives which can replace the main company scheme.

Expatriate pensions/employee

Used to describe the rather idiosyncratic arrangements companies make to provide pensions for employees who are seconded abroad. Other terms used for these employees include 'mobile employees', 'cross border employees' and, where the employee works for a foreign company and is sent overseas, 'third country nationals' (TCNs).

Expression of wish

A document, which is completed and sealed by the scheme member, that states to whom the member wants the death-in-service lump-sum benefit to be paid. The expression of wish form remains sealed until the member's death and, unless the instructions are clearly inappropriate, the trustees would normally abide by the member's wishes. The dependant's pension is usually only paid to a lawful spouse, although an increasing number of schemes will pay the pension to a common law partner, including same-sex partners.

External manager

An independent investment manager appointed to run the pension fund.

Final salary scheme

Links the value of the pension to earnings – usually at or around retirement. About 85 per cent of company schemes in the UK are final salary (in the US they are known as 'defined benefit' schemes). Typically the pension builds up at a rate of one-sixtieth of final salary for each year of service up to a maximum of forty-sixtieths or two-thirds final salary (subject to restrictions in the case of certain higher earners – *see* **earnings cap**). *See also* **money purchase**.

Financial Services Act 1986

The Act that set up the system of self-regulation for financial services. It is overseen by the **Financial Services Authority** (FSA).

Financial Services Authority (FSA)

The regulator for sales and marketing of retail life, pension and investment products.

Free-standing additional voluntary contributions (FSAVCs)

If your company pension is likely to fall short of the maximum two-thirds final salary set by the Revenue, it is possible to pay voluntary top-up contributions either to the company **additional voluntary contribution** (AVC) scheme or to a free-standing AVC (FSAVC). An FSAVC is an individual contract between the employee and the life office, whereas under the company AVC scheme the contract is between the individual and the trustees. *See also* **individual savings account (ISA).**

Funded and unfunded unapproved schemes

Pension schemes recognised by the Revenue but not approved for tax purposes. They are used to provide pension for employees caught by the **earnings cap**.

Gilts

Gilt-edged securities are Government bonds. Index-linked gilts are issued by the Government to provide interest payment and redemption proceeds that increase in line with inflation.

Group personal pension (GPP)

At its most basic, this is little more than a series of individual personal pension plans although if the employer sets up the group plan it is more likely to make a contribution and, perhaps, provide life assurance and other benefits on top. The GPP is not defined as an occupational scheme and so the same contribution and benefit limits as individual **personal pensions** apply.

Guaranteed equity funds

Funds that limit your exposure to falls in the stockmarket and provide a percentage of the gains. They do this by investing mainly in **gilts** and **cash** and then buying **derivatives** to provide the guarantees. Guaranteed funds may be worth considering for **income drawdown** plans but otherwise it is not clear whether long-term equity investors get value for money given the cost of the guarantee. Some commentators regard guaranteed funds as the natural replacement for **with-profits funds**.

Guaranteed minimum pension (GMP)

See **contracted out/contracted in**.

Ill-health pension

Awarded to members who are no longer able to continue employment due to chronic ill health. The calculation of the pension varies but generous schemes pay the amount the employee would have received had they stayed in employment until normal retirement date, at their current rate of pay.

Illustration/projection

Used by advisers and sales representatives to show you what your investment might be worth at maturity, assuming different rates of annual growth set by one of the industry's regulators, the Personal Investments Authority (PIA). Given that the growth rates are standard, the main purpose of an illustration is to show the impact of the life office's charges on your investment.

Income drawdown

A type of **personal pension** that allows you to keep your fund fully invested until age 75 before buying an annuity. You draw your retirement income directly from the fund. Too expensive and risky for most people. *See also* **phased retirement**.

Independent financial adviser (IFA)

Advisers that are not tied to any one life office but instead search the market to find the best product for your needs. Some are remunerated by commission from the life office on the sale of a product while others operate on a fee basis. Fee-based advisers are likely to be more 'independent' than some commission-based advisers whose choice of provider might be influenced by the commission available on a product sale.

Independent trustees

Trustees, usually with a professional background (lawyers, actuaries etc.) who are not connected with the employer or the fund's advisers. By law an independent trustee must be appointed to oversee the pension scheme when a company becomes insolvent, but can be used to resolve conflicts of interest on the trustee board.

Index tracking

See **passive investment management**.

Individual savings account (ISA)

Launched in April 1999, replacing personal equity plans (PEPs) and tax-exempt special savings accounts (TESSAs). An ISA is a tax-efficient wrapper for a range of investments including **equities**, **bonds** and collective funds (unit trusts, investment trusts and open-ended investment companies). You can also hold **cash**. Under the rules you can invest £5000 per annum in an ISA (£7000 in 1999–2000), including up to £1000 in deposits (£3000 in 1999–2000); and £1000 in life assurance funds. Well worth considering as an alternative to **AVCs/FSAVCs**.

Industry-wide scheme

Pension scheme based on a sector or industry rather than run by a single employer.

Inheritance tax

A tax on wealth passed on at death. The nil rate band is £231 000 in 1999–2000. Anything over this is taxed at 40 per cent, although gifts between husband and wife are exempt.

In-house managers

Investment managers employed directly by the **trustees** or sponsoring employer to run the pension fund's money.

Initial period

See **capital levy**.

Insured scheme

Sold by life offices who provide both the administration and investment management services in one package. *See* **self-administered scheme**.

Integration

Company pension schemes that are integrated with the **basic State pension** scheme do not provide a pension for the first slice of earnings up to the **lower earnings limit** (LEL) for **National Insurance**. The LEL is approximately £3500. Some schemes have a higher 'integration factor' of one-and-a-half or twice the LEL, so that there is no pension for the first £4750–£7000 of earnings.

Investment manager

A professional firm appointed by the **trustees** to carry out the day-to-day investment of the pension fund.

Investment trusts

British companies, quoted on the UK stock exchange, that invest in the shares of UK and overseas companies. Investment trusts have a fixed number of shares and the share price is determined partly by the value of the underlying assets and partly by supply and demand for the shares themselves. Several investment trusts now offer a **personal pension** plan.

Key features
The (supposedly) simple summary of the product you will receive before you sign up for an investment. The most important feature is the details on charges, but it should also include details on the risk level of the investment and the pattern of contributions to which you are committed.

Life office
A life assurance company authorised to sell life and pensions products. The term is also used to describe the life assurance arm of a composite insurer, that is one that sells life and pensions products and also general insurance such as household and motor cover. For reasons best known to itself, the UK financial services sector uses the term 'assurance' for life products and 'insurance' for general products. This book follows that terminology.

Lower earnings limit (LEL)
The threshold above which you pay National Insurance contributions – up to the upper earnings limit. In 1999–2000 the LEL is £66 per week and the UEL is £500 per week. The LEL is the lowest level of earnings taken into account for the **State Earnings-Related Pension Scheme** (SERPS).

Managed/mixed fund
Invests in a range of the manager's other main funds, usually including UK and overseas **equities**, **gilts**, **bonds** and, in some cases, **property**.

Married woman's stamp
More correctly, the 'reduced' rate of **National Insurance** contribution women can still pay provided they were married or widowed before 5 April 1977. The reduced rate does not build up an entitlement to the **basic State pension**, among other benefits.

Misappropriation
Where pension fund money (or any money for that matter) is put to wrong use by someone who does not own it. Theft to you and me.

Money purchase
Schemes that do not guarantee a pension linked to the member's final salary (also called **defined contribution** schemes). Instead contributions are invested to build up a fund that is used at retirement to buy an **annuity** from a life office. The annuity provides the guaranteed regular

income until death. Money purchase schemes can be contract in to the **State Earnings-Related Pension Scheme** (SERPS) (contracted-in money purchase scheme or CIMPS) or out (contracted-out money purchase scheme or COMPS). *See also* **contracted out/contracted in**.

Mutual life office

A life office that is effectively owned by its policyholders. Unlike a 'proprietary' company, it does not have shareholders.

National Insurance

A form of taxation levied on **band earnings** – earnings between the **lower earnings limit** and **upper earnings limits** (LEL and UEL). These are £66 and £500 per week in 1999–2000. The main rate for an employee earning over the UEL is 10 per cent.

National Insurance rebate

A partial return of **National Insurance** contributions is rebated to individuals who contract out of the **State Earnings-Related Pension Scheme** (SERPS) with an **appropriate personal pension**. The rebate varies from just over 3 per cent to 9 per cent, depending on age.

Net relevant earnings

Earnings on that **personal pension** contributions are based. Net relevant earnings are roughly equivalent to annual profits from any self-employed activities (after deducting losses and certain business charges on income) or annual earnings from employment where either there is no company pension scheme or you have chosen not to join the company pension scheme.

Non-pensionable employment

Earnings that are not already used as the basis for pension contributions. The term refers to employees whose employer does not provide a pension scheme (or where they do not join) and the self-employed.

Occupational Pensions Advisory Service (OPAS)

A free service for members of occupational schemes who have a complaint which the scheme trustees have not solved satisfactorily.

Occupational Pensions Regulatory Authority (OPRA)

A regulator for company pensions, established under the Pensions Act 1995. It took over from the Occupational Pensions Board in April 1997.

Occupational pension scheme

A scheme sponsored by an employer to provide relevant benefits to employees.

Offshore trusts

Where the pension fund is situated offshore – usually in the Channel Isles – to avoid certain taxes or to provide different benefits from the company's main scheme. Most often used by multinational employers to provide pensions for their **expatriate employees**.

Open market option

Your right at retirement to take the proceeds of your personal pension (or similar) and buy your **annuity** elsewhere. Annuity rates (the income you buy with your pension fund) vary considerably, so it is vital to shop around.

Opting out

Can either refer to employees who leave their company pension scheme or to those who leave the **State Earnings-Related Pension Scheme** (SERPS) in order to invest instead in a **personal pension**.

Passive investment management

Passive managers tend not to pick individual stocks on the basis of research but instead use computer models to do this for them, often making use of specific FT indices. Where the manager tries to emulate the performance of the index this is known as index tracking.

Pension

A long-term tax-efficient investment designed to provide an income in retirement and other related benefits such as life assurance.

Pension age

The age at which you can draw your pension from the State scheme, your company scheme or your individual plan. In company schemes it may be possible to take early retirement, in which case the pension is reduced to take account of the longer payment period and shorter accrual period.

Pension forecast

A useful service provided by the Department of Social Security that tells you what your State pension is worth.

Pensionable pay

Earnings on which the employee's contributions to a company scheme are based. Pensionable pay can be basic pay or gross pay. If it is basic pay then it will not include overtime or bonuses. However, it is possible to pay **additional voluntary contributions** (AVCs) or **free-standing AVCs** (FSAVCs) to provide a pension for these additional earnings.

Pensions Ombudsman

An independent arbitrator for pension disputes – usually referred by OPAS. The Ombudsman has statutory power to enforce decisions.

Performance measurement

Used to check how well or badly the investment manager has done. There are usually two measurements: first, against an industry average, and second, against a specific benchmark or target set by the **trustees** of the fund.

Personal pension

Introduced in July 1988, personal pensions replaced the old-style retirement annuity plans. Personal pensions can be used by the self-employed and employees who are not members of company pension schemes. The top-up version is used to supplement the **appropriate personal pension** which allows employees to contract out of the **State Earning-Related Pension Scheme** (SERPS) on an individual basis.

Phased retirement

Similar to **income drawdown**, phased retirement allows you to keep your pension fund fully invested until age 75.

Pooled pension fund

It is not economic for most individuals and smaller schemes to set up their own individually held portfolio of shares. Instead they purchase units in a fund that combines the investments of several schemes. Economies of scale reduce the cost of dealing, administration and custody, but the pension funds do not directly own the assets and the investment strategy is not set by the **trustees** but by the **investment manager**.

Professional adviser

Used to describe the firms of accountants, auditors, actuaries and solicitors who help run company pension schemes. Also used to describe the professionals who act as **independent financial advisers** for private clients.

Property

In the context of pension fund investment, property means the ownership of land and buildings that are used by businesses or other organisations which pay rent to the owner. Ownership is often on a collective basis.

Proprietary life office

Quoted companies that have share holders, unlike **mutual life offices** which are owned by their policyholders.

Protected rights

The fund that is built up from the rebates of **National Insurance** contributions under a **personal pension** and other types of **money purchase** pensions. The protected rights fund is restricted in the way it can be used, but the level of pension is not guaranteed – it is hard to see why the label 'protected' was attached except for marketing purposes.

Purchased life annuity (PLA)

See **annuity**.

Qualifying year

A complete tax year in which the full rate of **National Insurance** contribution was paid or credited. Qualifying years count towards your **basic state pension**.

Reduction in premium (RIP)

A method of showing the impact of charges on your investment. In this case the calculation shows the percentage of each premium lost in charges over the entire contract. *See also* **reduction in yield**.

Reduction in yield (RIY)

A method of showing the impact of the provider's charges on your investment. The RIY shows the equivalent annual percent charge over the entire contract. *See also* **reduction in premium**.

Regular premium

Any frequency of payment – most commonly monthly or annual – where you commit yourself to paying a certain amount at regular intervals for a fixed period. One of the main problems with regular contracts is that life offices usually pay all the commission to the adviser or salesman up front that would otherwise have been earned over the entire term. If the contract is terminated early then you will find that most of your money has disappeared in commission payments.

Renewal commission

Often overlooked by the consumer, the renewal commission is paid by the life office to the adviser at certain intervals throughout the contract.

Retirement annuity plan (RAP)

The predecessor of **personal pensions** and similar in most respects except that they did not allow individual employees to contract out of the **State Earnings-Related Pension Schemes** (SERPS). Neither could they accept an employer's contribution.

Segregated pension fund

Where the investment manager is hired by the **trustees** to follow a specific brief and constructs a separate portfolio of assets that are directly owned by the fund. *See also* **pooled pension fund**.

Self-administered scheme

Where the investment is run in-house or by a specialist firm of investment managers. 'Administered' actually refers to the investment function. Under most insured schemes the investment management and administration are both carried out by the same life office – although among the larger schemes this is changing. *See also* **insured scheme**.

Self-invested personal pensions (SIPPs)

Personal pensions that allow the individual to separate the administration and investment and therefore allow the individual to exercise much greater freedom in the investment choice. Only viable for larger investments.

State Earnings-Related Pension Scheme (SERPS)

Set up in 1978 to provide employees with a pension linked to average earnings between the lower and upper threshold for **National Insurance**. It will be replaced eventually by a flat-rate pension for low earners. At present employees are automatically in SERPS unless they have **contracted out** through a company pension scheme or **appropriate personal pension** plan.

Single premium/recurring single premium (SP/RSP)

A one-off contribution that does not lock you in to any future payments. If commission is paid to the adviser this also is on a one-off basis, so there are no financial penalties if you decide not to pay further contributions. Recurring single premiums should be treated as one-off payments for commission purposes, but do check this point.

Small self-administered schemes (SSAS)

Approved occupational pension schemes for small businesses which allow far more flexibility than standard schemes. For example, they include the facility to self-invest to a high degree and to take a loan from the fund. The maximum number of members is 12.

Specialist manager

Focuses on one specific asset class (European equities), type of stock (small companies) or geographical area (Latin America) among other specialist categories.

Stakeholder schemes

A low-cost group pension proposed by the Government which will operate as an **industry-wide scheme**. The Government will introduce rules so that stakeholders conform to certain standards on charges and flexible contract terms. The first schemes may be launched by April 2001.

Stock selection

The process where the **investment manager** chooses individual securities on the basis of research into the company's potential future prospects in the light of expected economic conditions.

Superannuation scheme

A Government-run pension scheme in the public sector.

Surplus

In pension fund terms, a surplus is identified if the fund is greater than that needed to pay the guaranteed benefits.

Tax-free cash

Under Inland Revenue rules it is possible to take part of your pension benefits at retirement in the form of tax-free cash. This process is known as 'commutation'. The maximum amount of tax-free cash varies according to the pension arrangement and when it started. As a rough guide, under **personal pensions** you can take up to 25 per cent of the fund (not including the **protected rights** element built up from rebates of **National Insurance** contributions), while under company schemes the maximum is usually one-and-a-half times salary (subject to restrictions in the case of certain higher earners – *see* **earnings cap**).

Transfer analysis

Before you transfer your pension benefits out of your company scheme your adviser should conduct a thorough transfer analysis to make sure that the full value of the company scheme is taken into account when comparing the benefits with a **personal pension** plan or the new employer's scheme.

Transfer value

The amount you take out of a pension scheme if you leave employment and want to transfer your pension benefits into the new employer's scheme or into an individual pension plan. Since company scheme membership is no longer a condition of employment, it is also possible, though usually unwise, to transfer out your benefits while still in the same employment.

Trust deed

The legal document on which a Revenue-approved **occupational pension scheme** is based. The use of a trust legally separates the pension fund from the rest of the company's assets and allows the **trustees** to manage the money on behalf of the beneficiaries.

Trustees

You can't have a trust without a trustee, who, as the legal owner of the fund, is obliged to look after the assets on behalf of the beneficiaries. Trustees can be drawn from the management team and from the scheme members.

Unapproved pension schemes

Schemes that are recognised by the Revenue but are not approved for tax purposes. Used mainly to top up benefits for employees caught by the **earnings cap**.

Unit-linked/unit trust pension funds

Instead of directly owning assets, in a unit-linked fund (sold by life offices) or unit trust fund your pension contributions buy units in a pooled fund. The performance of the units purchased with your contributions is directly linked to the performance of the underlying assets. Although similar in many respects, the charging structure of the unit-linked fund is more complex than the unit trust fund (although not necessarily more expensive) and may contain hidden costs if up-front commission is paid to an adviser.

Upper earnings limit

See **National Insurance**.

Waiver of premium

A vital insurance policy for a **regular premium** pension plan. If you are too ill to work the pension company credits your fund with contributions until retirement.

Winding up

The term used to explain the legal termination of a pension scheme. Details on how the scheme should be wound up, if it becomes necessary, are set out in the **trust deed** and rules.

With-profits/unitised with-profits pension funds

With-profits funds are invested in UK and overseas **equities**, **gilts**, **bonds** and **property**. Under a with-profits contract the life office provides a guaranteed minimum sum at maturity to which it adds annual or 'reversionary' bonuses which, once allocated, cannot be taken away. The annual bonuses are 'smoothed' to avoid volatility. On top of this there is a discretionary (not guaranteed) final or 'terminal' bonus which reflects recent performance of the with-profits fund. Unitised with-profits plans invest in the same type of fund but here your contributions buy units that can be bought and sold in the same way as a unit-linked plan. However, there is no guaranteed sum at maturity. It has to be said that the bonus systems and charging structures of traditional and unitised with-profits policies are ridiculously complicated.

Working life

Defined by the Department of Social Security for State pension purposes as 49 years for a man and 44 for a women (rising to 49 when the State pension age is equalised). Your right to the basic State pension depends on your **National Insurance** contribution record during your working life.

INDEX